Governance in the Social Economy

Ludger Kolhoff

Governance in the Social Economy

An Introduction

Springer

Ludger Kolhoff
Ostfalia Hochschule Braunschweig
Wolfenbüttel, Germany

ISBN 978-3-658-38742-6 ISBN 978-3-658-38743-3 (eBook)
https://doi.org/10.1007/978-3-658-38743-3

Responsible Editor: Katrin Emmerich
This Springer imprint is published by the registered company Springer Fachmedien Wiesbaden GmbH, part of Springer Nature.
The registered company address is: Abraham-Lincoln-Str. 46, 65189 Wiesbaden, Germany
(www.springer.com/mycopy)

Preface

The term governance is on everyone's lips. If you enter the term in Amazon, you will get more than 100,000 results[1]. But what does this term mean? Benz et al. understand governance to be new forms of coordination between actors whose actions are interdependent, that is, they can support or impair each other (Benz et al., 2007, 9). So governance is about regulating something together. The term is derived from the Latin *gubernare* (steer the rudder, guide, lead) or the French *gouverner* (manage, lead, educate). In English, *governance* is understood to mean "the action or manner of governing" (Oxford Dictionary).

Governance is "the totality of the many ways in which individuals as well as public and private institutions regulate their common affairs. It is a continuous process through which controversial or different interests are reconciled and cooperative action can be initiated. The term includes both formal institutions and authority systems with enforcement power as well as informal rules that are agreed upon or considered to be in their own interest by people and institutions […]." Definition of the UN Commission on Global Governance, quoted after Stiftung Entwicklung und Frieden 1995: 4 et seq. http://www.bpb.de/veranstaltungen/netzwerke/teamglobal/67464/definition

The discussion about governance is gaining importance as known control and regulation forms, from which one generally expects the solution of problems in modern society, "that is, the state or the hierarchical model in politics, administration and companies, the market or associations and social communities, have become problematic" (Benz et al., 2007, 9). Modern societies are characterized by a variety of network-like structures and negotiation systems that are formed by

[1]As of March 2021.

state and non-state actors. State, market and civil society interact with their different steering mechanisms or -logics. (The state steering mechanisms or logics is the law, the market is oriented towards the means of exchanging money and in civil society it is negotiated.)

Negotiation processes in economics and political science have gained in importance, and since, in the social economy, resources are negotiated politically while the social is managed, governance aspects are of general importance. In Chap. 1, the two main sources of the governance discussion, "economy" and "political science", are considered in more detail. In general, a distinction is made between the three governance levels: macro (Chap. 2), meso (Chap. 3) and micro level (Chap. 4). Chap. 2, first looks at the macro level of governance with the three "orders of governance" (first, second and third). The meso level ("cooperation", coordination, control and control forms of social enterprises) is discussed in Chap. 3, and the micro level ("interactions") in Chap. 4, which is about actor relationships and interaction mechanisms.

For the sake of better readability, this book uses the generic masculine form for the most part. This always implies both forms, thus also includes the female form.

Contents

About the Author

Prof. Dr. phil. Ludger Kolhoff Year of birth 1957, studied pedagogy, electrical engineering and political science in Berlin (First Technical-Scientific State Examination, Magister Examination, Promotion to Dr. phil.). From 1979 to 1984 he was managing director and special representative for self-help projects of the Martinswerk e. V. (member of the Diakonisches Werk) in Berlin. After the study referee (Second Technical-Scientific State Examination) he worked in Berlin from 1986 to 1993 as study councillor at a vocational school for students with special needs, and from 1983 to 1993 he was also chairman of the supervisory board and expert advisory board of the Sanierungstreuhand- und Beschäftigungsträger "Stattbau Stadtentwicklungs-GmbH", and from 1991 to 1993 founding managing director of the "Perspektive, Gesellschaft für Bauberatung und Betreuung mbH", a subsidiary of the Paritätischer Wohlfahrtsverband (Landesverband Berlin) and the Stattbau GmbH. Since 1993 he is professor at the Faculty of Social Work of the Ostfalia University of Applied Sciences in Braunschweig-Wolfenbüttel and represents the subject area of social management tasked with priorities organisation/organisational development/project management, financing, personnel management as well as start-up and company founding. Since 2001 he heads the Master's program in Social Management. He is chairman of the Bundesarbeitsgemeinschaft Sozialmanagement/Sozialwirtschaft an Hochschulen (BAG SMW) e. V.

Sources of the Governance Discussion 1

Abstract

According to the basic definition, governance includes various forms of control and regulation of different actors who are in a dependent relationship with each other, that is, they do not act autonomously, but can support or affect each other. The roots of the governance discussion can be found in both economics and political science. These two sources of the governance discussion are to be considered in more detail.

Learning Objectives

A deeper understanding should be developed of what can be included in governance. First, it will be conveyed that the use of the term governance must be considered in different contexts.

1.1 Economy

Transaction cost economics, founded by Oliver Williamson as part of the new institutional economics, compares the efficiency of institutional arrangements in which economic transactions take place. It is based on the assumption that every trade, every form of exchange is associated with costs. For example, before the contract is concluded, information costs may arise in order to ascertain prices and qualities, further negotiation costs, costs for the preparation of the contract, expert opinion, etc., and after conclusion expenses for control and enforcement arise, for example in connection with the transfer and enforcement of disposal rights.

L. Kolhoff, *Governance in the Social Economy*,
https://doi.org/10.1007/978-3-658-38743-3_1

Furthermore, if necessary, post-contractual and adaptation costs for errors and controls, e.g., quality controls, must be taken into account. Transactions are efficient when the actors choose a form of coordination in which the transaction costs are minimal. Therefore, the goal of transaction cost economics is to examine schemes of institutional coordination of transactions (Benz & Dose, 2010, p. 17 et seq.).

"Governance" is, according to Williamson, the term for institutional regulations of action coordination. And these rules do not always lead to the market, because the costs of economic transactions are not necessarily lowest when transactions are settled via a market (Benz et al., 2007, p. 11). Instead, hierarchies or networks seem to be superior. The criterion for selection of the appropriate "governance mode" is the level of transaction costs (Williamson, 1990, p. 78 et seq.).

Transactions are efficient when they are organized in such a way that they have low costs. In doing so, certain properties of the transactions under consideration (factor specificity) are important, such as their "frequency" and "uncertainty" as well as the specificity of the investments required in human and physical capital, i.e., qualifications, knowledge and reputation ("human specificity") or location ("location specificity") and production-specific facilities ("physical specificity").

In the case of low factor specificity, i.e., when specific capital is not or only to a limited extent required for the transaction, market-based processing should take place. It is suitable for simple, uncomplicated transactions (Fig. 1.1).

However, if specific investments are significant, it is advisable to involve the transaction relationship in an institutional manner, for example, by means of long-term contracts (e.g., cooperation contracts).

In the case of very highly specific investments, integration into the corporate hierarchy is advisable.

Example: Newspaper

An example is the newspaper, which only fulfills its function if it is ready at breakfast time. For this reason, the printing press is centrally positioned in relation to the newspaper publisher and usually owned by the publisher. In contrast, the quality of its own output is separable from that of an input that is positioned peripherally. Thus, a book publisher can negotiate with different printers and reject a bad offer. Therefore, book publishers usually do not own printing presses, but contract via the market.

Source: http://wirtschaftslexikon.gabler.de/Definition/transaktionskostenoekonomik.html. Accessed: 25.05.2019.

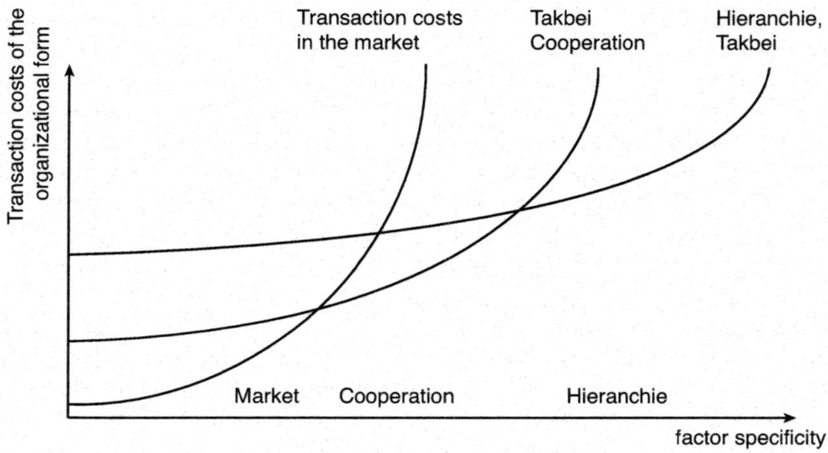

Fig. 1.1 Transaction costs of organizational forms. (Source: http://edoc.hu-berlin.de/dissertationen/dienel-wolfram-2000-12-07/HTML/dienel-ch2.html. Accessed: 22.06.2019)

Technological changes, in particular the use of new information technologies, make it possible to reduce transaction costs and promote a shift to organizational and institutional networks, e.g., in the automotive industry (Sydow, 1992; Garcia Sanz et al., 2007), but also in other sectors (Sydow, 2010). Accordingly, Castells concludes that many "business enterprises and increasingly also organizations and institutions […] are organized in networks with variable geometry, the interlocking of which replaces the traditional distinction between corporations and small businesses, extends across all sectors and along which different geographical concentrations of economic units expands" (Castells, 2017, p. 569).

The network idea has also spread to the social economy (Schubert, 2018), because its structures are complex and cooperative networks are often superior to market-oriented or administrative coordination and control patterns.

1.2 Political Science

In political science, governance is understood as the opposite of state-hierarchical government—"the system by which a state or community is governed" (Benz et al., 2007, p. 11).

Government takes place "top down" within the framework of formal, fixed procedures and fixed institutionalizations in hierarchies and bureaucracies, and it is characterized by the conflict regulation pattern of power.

Governance, on the other hand, takes place within the framework of negotiation processes, accords and agreements, within networks and cooperation. It is about arrangements in configurations where there is no single absolutely dominant actor.

Examples can be found at the level of international relations, because beyond the nation state, governing in the classical mode of hierarchical control is not possible at all (Mayntz, 2010, p. 37). Here we find a "governance without government" (Benz et al., 2007, p. 12). The negotiation processes at the international level, for example in the UN or in the European Union, in which formal and informal approaches interact (hearings, lobbying and negotiations), are well known. That a hierarchy is not necessary in order to enable action coordination between states is shown by the example of the conclusion of the "CETA free trade agreement" between the European Union and Canada. The phases mandate, negotiations and decision are carried out.

1. **Mandate**

   The governments of the EU countries mandate the Commission to negotiate. (In this case, the national governments of the European Commission give the mandate to negotiate CETA in June 2013.)
2. **Negotiations**

   The representatives of the EU negotiate with the representatives of Canada, exchange written proposals and draft a text of several hundred pages. Once the negotiations are concluded, the negotiated text is published on the internet.

3. **Decision**

The text is forwarded to the governments of the EU Member States and the European Parliament. The national governments and the European Parliament decide whether to conclude the agreement.

Governance structures can be found on different levels of the European Union. The EU is not a sovereign state because it does not exercise sole sovereignty, but rather an overall system of European institutions, nation states and regions. Governance in the EU is a coordination and negotiation process in which nation states and regions, the Commission, the European Parliament and a variety of non-state actors are involved. Public officials and representatives of societal interests work together. Hierarchy (control through law), negotiations and policy competition are combined on different levels (Fig. 1.2).

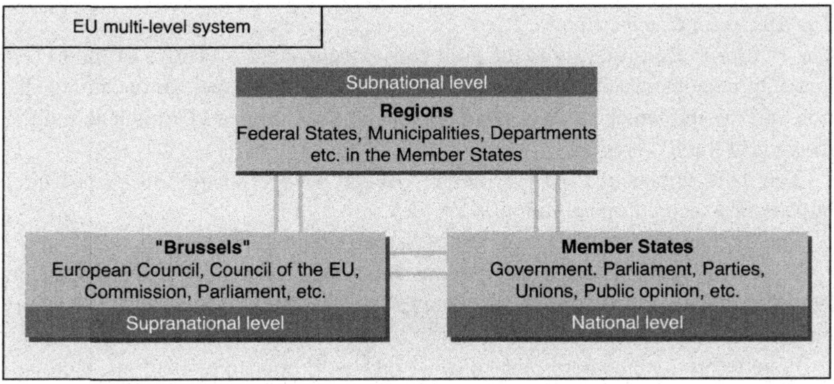

Fig. 1.2 EU multi-level system. (Source: http://www.onlinedissertation.de/europaeische_union/problem/komplexitaet.htm)

Member States are represented in EU institutions such as the European Council and the Council (Council of Ministers), which work in conjunction with the European Parliament and the European Commission.

The main organs of the EU and their cooperation are briefly outlined below.

The European Council
Four times a year, the heads of state or government of the EU meet to set the political agenda of the EU. The European Council is the highest level of political cooperation between EU countries.

Council of the EU (Council of Ministers)
In the Council of the EU (Council of Ministers), ministers from all EU countries meet to discuss, amend and adopt legislation. They also coordinate their policy areas. All ministers present at the Council meetings are authorised by the member states' governments to act with binding legal force.

The European Parliament
The European Parliament is the legislative body of the EU. It is elected directly by the citizens of the EU every five years and, in addition to its legislative function (adoption of EU legislation in cooperation with the Council of the EU on the basis of proposals from the European Commission), has a supervisory function over all EU institutions. The European Parliament, together with the Council of the EU, sets the EU budget.

The European Commission
The European Commission is the politically independent executive of the EU. It is solely responsible for the preparation of proposals for new European legislation and the implementation of the decisions of the European Parliament and the Council of the EU.

The main organs of the EU (Source: Official website of the European Union https://europa.eu/european-union/index_de)

The interaction of the main organs is visualized in figure (1.3).

Thus, the member states and regions have the opportunity to participate in European decision-making, while there is also a feedback of European provisions on national and regional levels.

In addition to mandatory mechanisms, such as European regulations, there are also non-binding instruments. They work through "soft governance tools" (Milotay, 2017, p. 6), such as the open coordination method (Yollu-Tok, 2016), which

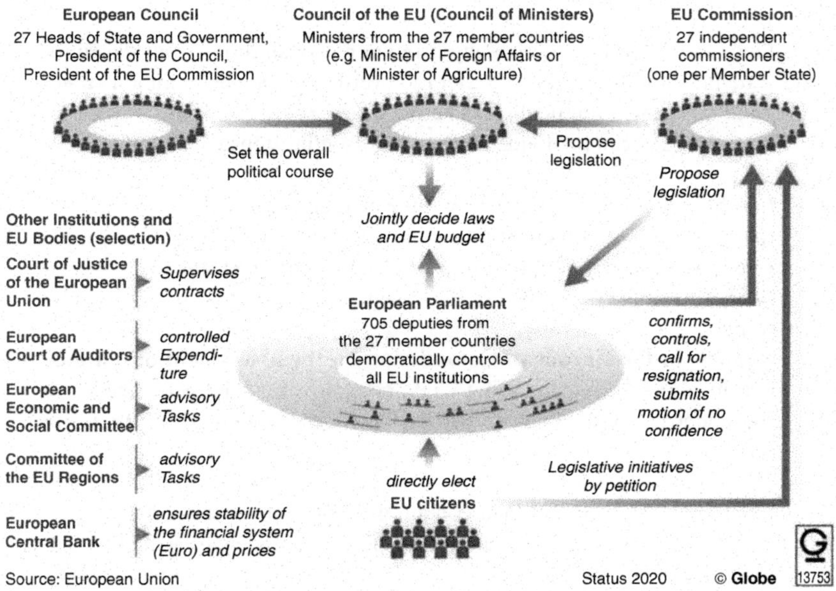

Fig. 1.3 Interaction of the main organs of the EU. (Source Globus Infographic 13753)

is used to set common goals in the areas of employment, social protection, education, youth and training, and to review them through methods such as peer learning or peer counseling (Milotay, 2017, p. 7), thus harmonizing different national structures.

The "Open Coordination Method"

Via the "open coordination method", EU-prescribed strategic political guidelines are implemented into national law without having to intervene directly in the responsibilities of the Member States. The open coordination method can be described as a kind of "non-binding law". It is a form of intergovernmental policy-making that does not lead to binding EU legislative measures and does not impose the introduction or amendment of laws on EU countries. For this reason, the approach is also referred to as "soft law".

Since the EU cannot derive any original responsibilities from the European treaties, this approach is a tool to nevertheless pursue common strategies and implement political goals across Europe.

The approach can be divided into three essential steps:

1. **Establishment of guidelines by the European Council** (partly provided with quantitative and qualitative indicators)
2. **Creation of national action plans by the Member States** (including bilateral talks for improvement in the run-up to the Joint Report)
3. **Reports of the European Commission on the assessment of national action plans** ("Benchmarking", i.e., comparison of the performance of EU countries, and exchange of best practices, monitored by the Commission).

The National Action Plans each contain examples of "best practice"—particularly exemplary implementation models—with a view to achieving certain policy goals. The Joint Report of the Commission, in which National Action Plans are evaluated and the examples of "best practice" are also included, is intended to ensure comparability between Member States. At the same time, this is supposed to initiate a mutual learning process in the European Union. This open method of coordination provides new framework conditions for cooperation between EU countries. Its purpose is to align national policy with the achievement of certain common goals. In this form of intergovernmental cooperation, the EU countries assess each other ("conformity pressure"); the Commission is limited to monitoring the process. The European Parliament and the European Court of Justice are only marginally involved in the OMC. (Source: https://eur-lex.europa.eu/summary/glossary/open_method_coordination.html?locale=de)

Governance is not only a political fact at the EU level. For Benz, Lütz, Schimank, Simonis, the term "governance" describes "the reality of governing and collective action in societies in which the boundaries of the state have long since dissolved both in relation to society and in relation to the international environment" (Benz et al., 2007, p. 11). For them, the term refers to "new modes of social or political steering and coordination in complex constellations of actors and

Table 1.1 Differences of Government and Governance

Government	Governance
• is firmly institutionalized	• is flexible
• is formal	• is informal
• takes place "top down" within the framework of fixed procedures and firm institutionalization	• is self-regulating
• has a high density of regulation; it is about fixed procedures	• has a low density of regulation; things are not strongly limited

interorganizational structures" (Benz et al., 2007, p. 11). No completely new phenomena are described by the term *governance*. Instead, changes that have already taken place or are still taking place are added to it.

Benz characterizes the following core concept of governance:

1. "Governance means steering and coordinating (or governing) with the aim of managing interdependencies between (usually) collective actors."
2. Steering and coordinating are based on institutionalized rule systems that are supposed to guide the actions of the actors, usually in combination with different rule systems (market hierarchy, majority rule, negotiation rules).
3. Governance also includes interaction patterns and modes of collective action that arise within institutions (networks, coalitions, contractual relationships, mutual adaptation in competition).
4. Processes of steering or coordinating as well as interaction patterns that the concept of governance wants to capture usually go beyond organizational boundaries, but also beyond the boundaries of state and society, which have become fluid in political practice. "Policy in this sense normally takes place in the interaction of state and non-state actors (or of actors within and outside of organizations)," says Benz, 2004, p. 23.

Government and governance structures exist side by side and can be distinguished from each other as shown in Table 1.1.

The criticism of governance structures, which can "overform" democratic structures, should be mentioned. This happens because in governance, political decisions can be made by people who have no political mandate and "whose work largely escapes the control of elected parliaments" (Roß, 2018, p. 732).

1.3 Review Questions for Chap. 1

1.1 What do you understand by transaction costs?
1.2 How is governance distinguished from government in political science?

References

Benz, A. (Hrsg.). (2004). *Governance – Regieren in komplexen Regelsystemen* (1. Aufl.). VS Verlag.

Benz, A., & Dose, N. (2010). Governance – Modebegriff oder nützliches sozialwissenschaftliches Konzept. In A. Benz & N. Dose (Hrsg.), *Governance – Regieren in komplexen Regelsystemen* (2., aktualisierte und veränderte Aufl., S. 13–36). VS Verlag.

Benz, A., Lütz, S., Schimank, U., & Simonis, G. (Hrsg.). (2007). *Handbuch Governance.* VS Verlag.

Castells, M. (2017). *Der Aufstieg der Netzwerkgesellschaft. Das Informationszeitalter, Wirtschaft, Gesellschaft, Kultur, Band. 1* (2. Aufl.). Springer VS.

Garcia Sanz, F. J., Semmler, K., & Walther, J. (Hrsg.). (2007). *Die Automobilindustrie auf dem Weg zur globalen Netzwerkkompetenz. Effiziente und flexible Supply Chains erfolgreich gestalten.* Springer-Verlag.

Mayntz, R. (2010). Governance im modernen Staat. In A. Benz & N. Dose (Hrsg.), *Governance – Regieren in komplexen Regelsystemen* (2., aktualisierte und veränderte Aufl., S. 37–48). VS Verlag.

Milotay, N. (2017). Social governance in the European Union. Governing complex systems. European Parliamentary Research Service PE 614.579, https://www.europarl.europa.eu/RegData/etudes/IDAN/2017/614579/EPRS_IDA(2017)614579_EN.pdf. Accessed: 18. Apr. 2021.

Roß, P. S. (2018). Governance. In K. Grunwald & A. Langer (Hrsg.), *Sozialwirtschaft. Handbuch für Wissenschaft und Praxis* (S. 726–738). Nomos.

Schubert, H. (2018). *Netzwerkorientierung in Kommune und Sozialwirtschaft.* Springer VS.

Sydow, J. (1992). *Strategische Netzwerke: Evolution und Organisation.* Gabler.

Sydow, J. (Hrsg.). (2010). *Management von Netzwerkorganisationen: Beiträge aus der „Managementforschung“* (5., aktualisierte Aufl.). Gabler.

Williamson, O. E. (1990). *Die ökonomischen Institutionen des Kapitalismus.* Mohr.

Yollu-Tok, A. (2016). Von der „Europäischen Beschäftigungsstrategie“ zur „offenen Methode der Koordinierung“ im Bereich der Sozialpolitik. In P. Hammerschmidt, U. Köttler, & J. Sagebiel (Hrsg.), *Die Europäische Union und die Soziale Arbeit* (1. Aufl., S. 79–97). AG SPAK.

Macro Level: "Orders of Governance" 2

Abstract

In the following chapter, the focus is on the macro level of the First, Second and Third Order of Governance. The First-Order of Governance is dedicated to political and economic negotiation and problem-solving processes, which take place in the social economy, especially at the local and regional level. The Second-Order of Governance refers to institutional framework conditions and the Third-Order of Governance considers normative framework conditions.

Learning Objectives

Using local and regional political and economic negotiation and problem-solving processes (First Order of Governance), the text illustrates how actors can cooperate in a social space. It is shown that the provision of social services by a state depends on both state and non-state actors who cooperate with each other in complex structures (Second Order of Governance). The importance of normative guidelines, i.e., binding rules and standards, of "Good Governance" (Third Order of Governance) is highlighted.

L. Kolhoff, *Governance in the Social Economy*,
https://doi.org/10.1007/978-3-658-38743-3_2

2.1 First Order of Governance, Problems and Opportunities: Local and Regional Problem-Solving and Policy Processes

In many political debates and crises, such as those surrounding the refugee issue in 2015/2016, space-related problems and their solutions (Kooimann, 2003, 135 et seq.) are at the center of attention.

International, national, regional and local processes have become increasingly interconnected, whether in the context of global governance at the level of the United Nations, European governance at the European level, national governance at the national level, regional governance at the level of regions or federal states, or local governance at the municipal level. What all approaches have in common is that they describe difficult-to-coordinate power and influence structures that are not based on a "top-down mentality" (Greca, 2005, p. 55), with both positive and negative effects. As an example, Greca cites lobbyists who expand their power at the local level by manipulating public contracts, or non-profit organizations and associations that assert their interests from below, that is, "bottom up" (Greca, 2005).

Since the social economy is particularly important at the local and regional levels, these will be presented below.

2.1.1 Local Governance

Local Governance refers to political and problem-solving processes at the municipal level. They are of high importance to the social economy because social work takes place on site. Consequently, the providers of social work have a strong local connection. For example, the independent cities and districts are the local public providers of youth (Section 69 (3) of the Social Code Book VIII) and social assistance (Section 3 (2) of the Social Code Book XII) and free providers, too, work at the local level and cooperate with public providers, parties, associations, companies and the actors of the informal sector within the meaning of Local Governance. Even actors of civil society can be addressed more easily at this level because here one can build on experiences in parish communities, committees or clubs. The municipal level offers the most opportunities to directly intervene in decision-making processes (Bogumil & Holtkamp, 2004, p. 145).

The "Social City" Program

An example of supporting Local Governance structures is the "Social City" program. It was launched in 1999 as a joint program of the federal government and the states and "stands for the attempt to institutionalize a more socially oriented urban development policy in order to bundle resources and cooperation in urban problem areas" (Häußermann & Walther, 2018, p. 2197).

The program led to a restructuring of urban development subsidies, which were linked to other fields relevant to urban development (Bogumil & Holtkamp, 2004, p. 154) because it is not only about buildings, but also about improving infrastructure for children, adolescents, old people and other target groups. Furthermore, it addresses questions such as employment promotion and improvement of living conditions on site as well as the promotion of lively neighborhoods and the strengthening of integration and social cohesion.

A total of approximately 5.3 billion euros had been provided by 2018 (BMI, 2019). The distribution of federal funds is visualized in the figure (2.1).

The "Social City" program is an example of how governance structures can be used, because the prerequisite and guarantee for its successful implementation are the involvement and participation of residents and social actors, such as representatives of schools, employment agencies, housing companies, etc., as well as strategic, cross-sectoral administrative action. Therefore, the municipalities commit themselves to building local networks and creating participatory structures in disadvantaged urban areas, in which experts discuss building and social measures with residents. Here, citizens actively bring their wishes and ideas, and the experts then develop action concepts as a template for policy and administration.

Coordination, steering and implementation groups were set up to control the process, as illustrated by the example of Munich Hasenbergl in Fig. 2.2.

Coordination Group

The Koordinierungsgruppe Hasenbergl (KGH) was the local committee that controlled work in the district, decided on the funding of small projects and coordinated all measures of the "Social City" program in Hasenbergl. It consisted of representatives of the district facilities, the competent specialist departments and the district committee.

Management was the responsibility of the Department of Town Planning and Building Regulation, Division III—Urban Renewal and Housing.

The tasks of the coordination group were:

- Networking of actors and activities in Hasenbergl
- Providing a forum for discussion of current topics and project ideas

- Development of components of the integrated action concept for a district strategy/district development
- Ensuring forms of participation for the district's residents (round tables, expert forums, large group events, etc.)
- vigorous public relations work in the district
- Prioritization/decision-making on project applications or their forwarding to the steering group

After the active phase of the "Social City" program has ended, the Bezirksausschuss 24 will take over responsibility and moderation for the program's continuation. To this end, the Bezirksausschuss has set up its own subcommittee on the Social City. In future, the task of coordinating the work of the group at the city level will be carried out by four working groups:

- Working Group on Business and Housing
- Working Group on Schools/Education
- Working Group on Community Activities, Culture, Health
- Working Group on REGSAM/Social Affairs

The Steering Group

In order to coordinate and steer the "Social City" program city-wide, a cross-departmental steering group (LGS) for the "Social City" was set up in accordance with the **Resolution of 21.07.1999**. This steering group has a permanent and an extended group of participants. It meets every four to six weeks and accompanies and controls the city-wide implementation of the "Social City" program in the areas being developed.

The management and chairmanship of the LGS lies with the Department of Urban Planning and Building Regulations, Main Department III—Urban Renewal and Housing. The chairmanship lies with Mr. Walter Buser (Department of Urban Planning and Building Regulations). If necessary, other municipal departments as well as other offices and experts are invited.

The regular participants are:

- Department of Urban Planning and Building Regulations, Division I—Urban Development Planning
- Department of Urban Planning and Building Regulations, Division III—Urban Renewal and Housing

- Social Welfare Department, Social Reporting/Social Planning
- Department of Labour and Economics, Municipal Employment Policy/ Qualification
- Health and Environmental Protection Department, Planning/Coordination
- School and Education Department, Planning/Coordination/Controlling
- Cultural Affairs Department, Infrastructure
- Construction Department, Division of Horticulture/Division of Architecture

Implementation Groups

The implementation groups were created as a result of the future conference in May 2001. There, topics most important to citizens were worked out.

The implementation groups provided the framework for the citizens' topical participation in the sense of the integrated action concept.

The Department of Urban Planning and Building Regulations and the Quarter Coordinators moderated the implementation groups and supported project ideas that arose from them. The integration into the coordination group resulted in mutual information and networking within the program.

Project groups

In addition to the implementation groups, there were so-called project groups for some specific projects in the following areas:

- Public relations
- Website of the district
- Wintersteinstraße residential area design
- Adventure playground Feldmochinger Anger
- Citizen participation

The organizational structure can be visualized as follows:

The "Social City" program is intended to contribute to the testing of new integrated policy forms at the local level. The central instrument is an integrated development concept that is to contain measures "serving to improve the housing and working conditions as well as the creation and preservation of socially stable resident structures" (171e para. 4 BauGB).

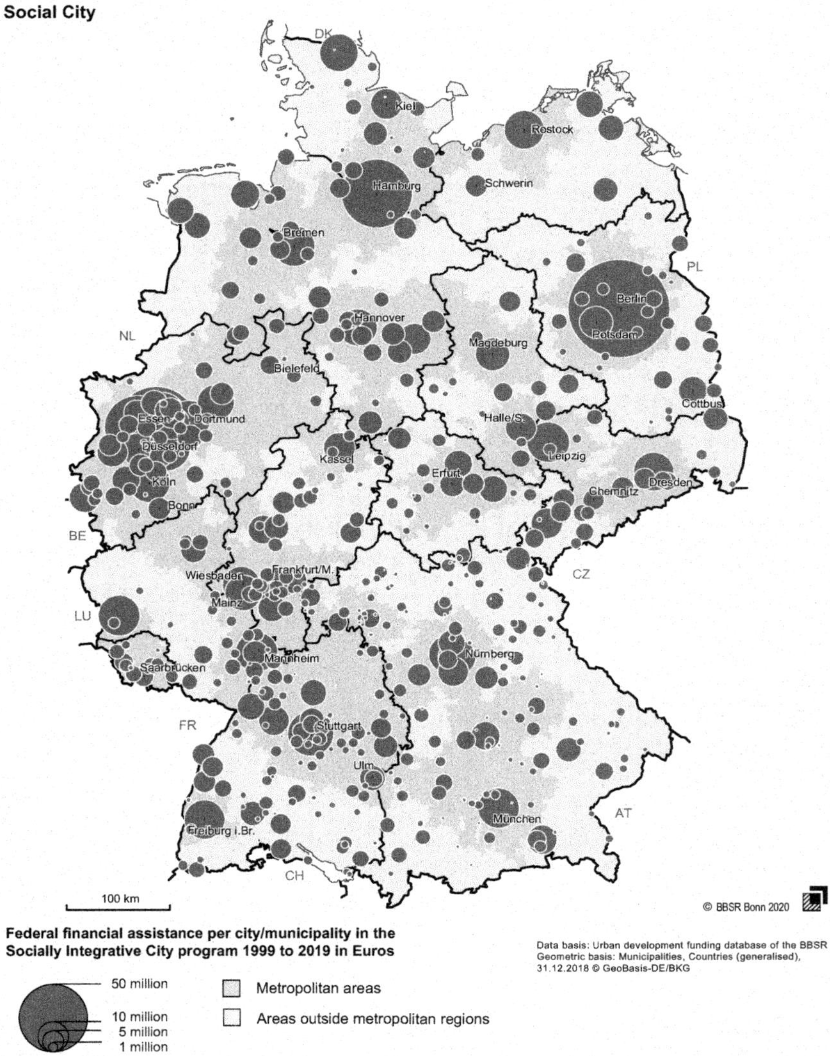

Fig. 2.1 Federal financial assistance per city/municipality in the "Social City" program 1999 to 2019 in Euros (BMI, 2021)

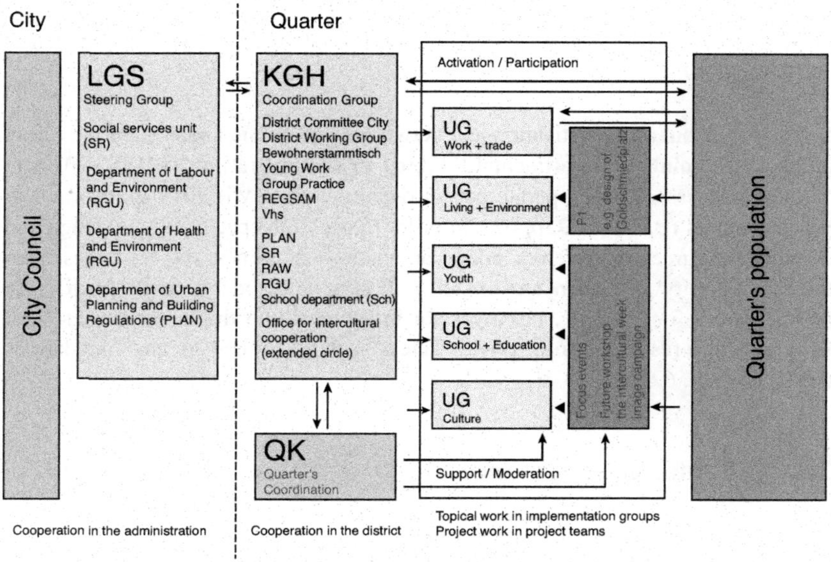

Fig. 2.2 Organisational structure of the "Social City" program using the example of Munich Hasenbergl http://www.sozialestadt-muenchen.de/index.php?option=com_content&view=article&id=51&Itemid=282

Inclusion and networking of a large number of public and non-public actors are important success factors here. The following instruments are used for this:

- "Integrated planning" and involving residents and relevant actors (BMI, 2019, p. 58).
- "Activate residents" and make them participants (BMI, 2019, p. 66).
- "Manage neighborhoods", i.e., inform, involve, activate and include the population; network and control relevant actors (BMI, 2019, p. 64).
- "Forge alliances", i.e., "combine tasks of the public sector with the commitment of welfare associations, clubs, churches, initiatives, companies and foundations as well as residents" (BMI, 2019, p. 70).

- "Share resources communally", i.e., use the instrument of the disposal fund to give actors on the ground the opportunity to implement projects independently (BMI, 2019, p. 68).

Just as important as the activation and networking of public and non-public actors is the overcoming of departmental thinking in administrations (BBSR, 2020, p. 55). It is necessary to cooperate across departments (BMI, 2019, p. 60) and to pool resources (BMI, 2019, p. 62). In order to use both specialist knowledge and financial resources of different policy areas and disciplines, the resources from the "Social City" program are linked with state and federal funds from other policy areas—for example, resources for integration into the labor market—and EU funds and resources from private actors such as companies and foundations (BMI, 2019, p. 62).

2.1.2 Regional Governance

The regional governance approach comes to us from the English-speaking world (Fürst, 2007, p. 353) and is most developed there, where the regional level is weakly organized. In England, there are neither regional associations nor government districts that can coordinate regional policy. A similar trend can be observed in Germany. For example, the government districts were abolished in Lower Saxony. At the same time, however, Europeanization is putting increasing demands on regional coordination. Consequently, it is necessary to make the regional level capable of strategy. Where regional government structures are lacking, an attempt is made within the framework of regional governance to coordinate regional processes and to involve state and non-state levels and actors that are important for the region. The term *region* refers to an area below a federal state but above a municipality or city. Within the scope of the regional governance concept, regions are action spaces defined by certain space-related functions, e.g., regional employment policy, economic development, regional cultural policy, etc. (Benz, 2004, p. 23). Here, governance means self-regulation in negotiations and networks of regional actors, municipalities, state actors, representatives of the economy, etc.

An example of supporting regional governance processes is the International Building Exhibition "Emscher Park" (Fig. 2.3).

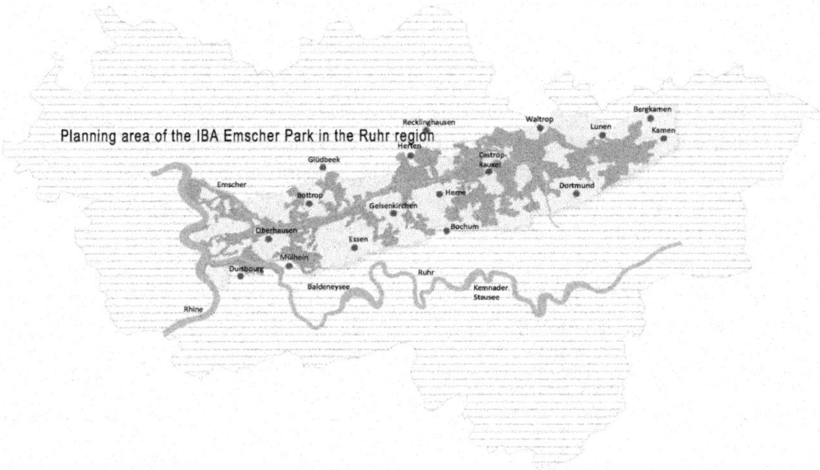

Fig. 2.3 Planning area of the IBA Emscher Park. (source: https://www.stiftung-deutscher-architekten.de/meldungen/detail/s-m-burggraef-dissertation-zur-iba-emscher-park/. Accessed:10.9.2021)

International Building Exhibition "Emscher Park"

17 cities (Bergkamen, Bochum, Bottrop, Castrop-Rauxel, Dortmund, Duisburg, Essen, Gelsenkirchen, Gladbeck, Herne, Herten, Kamen, Lünen, Mülheim an der Ruhr, Oberhausen, Recklinghausen, Waltrop) and two districts (Recklinghausen and Unna), located in an old industrial region on the river Emscher, with a total of 2.5 million inhabitants, have joined forces within the framework of the IBA Emscher Park from 1989 to 1999 to develop their region and make it more attractive.

The IBA Emscher Park succeeded as a regionalization process. "Today it is hardly worth mentioning if a Bochum city councillor is present at the city council meeting in the neighbouring town of Essen and the topic is the designation of commercial areas. Certain projects could only be tackled together if they affected the development of the entire metropolitan area" (Arnig, 2008).

Another example can be found in the Stuttgart region:

Stuttgart Region

In 1994, the regional association "Stuttgart region" emerged from the Stuttgart municipal association, which is legally very similar to the administrative unit, but whose task lies in regional development control.

The following tasks were assigned to the association by law:

- Regional planning,
- Landscape planning,
- Regional traffic planning,
- Economic development,
- Public local transport,
- Parts of waste disposal,
- Tourism marketing.

The concept of the "Stuttgart region" consists of three parts in which cooperation between regional actors takes place:

1. The responsibility for the arrangement of municipal planning
2. The connection of planning and expert responsibilities
3. The establishment of a democratically legitimate regional parliament

Source: http://www.bbsr.bund.de/BBSR/DE/Veroeffentlichungen/IzR/2003/Downloads/8_9Benz.pdf;jsessionid=89E50DC464550A48D8F55C6663C6CB57.live2053?__blob=publicationFile&v=2. Accessed: 22.02.2019

The special feature of Regional Governance are regional forms of self-regulation, which are based on voluntariness.

Fürst asks,

- how rule systems emerge that are not institutionally connected to each other,
- how rule systems are sanctioned,
- how actors form collectives capable of strategy and action,
- how the results of such self-regulation are integrated into legitimate political structures and
- how the jointly desired is also implemented (Fürst, 2004, p. 48).

Not every regional cooperation can be referred to as Regional Governance. In the context of regional self-regulation (e.g., the assumption of tasks of youth work in municipalities), state actors act, while in the case of Regional Governance, state

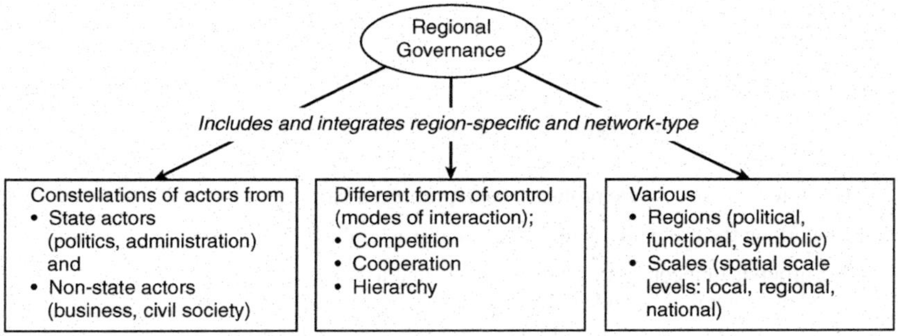

Fig. 2.4 Features of regional governance,

and non-state actors cooperate in networks. In contrast to state control, which is based on closed catchment areas, Regional Governance comprises complex control of regional structures.

The features of regional governance are outlined in the following figure (2.4):

Source: http://www.bbsr.bund.de/BBSR/DE/Veroeffentlichungen/IzR/2003/Downloads/8_9Benz.pdf?__blob=publicationFile&v=2. Accessed: 10.9.2021

In order to strengthen trust, solidarity, public interest orientation and willingness to cooperate through regional governance, the actors in the region (politicians, business representatives, association representatives, etc.) must be won over and moved to take joint action. There is no set rulebook; at best, there are patterns that need to be recognized. For this purpose, a checklist is helpful (see Table 2.1). It has been developed to capture regional governance patterns. The more questions can be answered with yes, the clearer the share of regional governance.

2.2 Second Order of Governance, Institutions: Institutional Aspects

In second approximation (Second Order of Governance), institutional aspects are addressed.

2.2.1 Governance and Welfare Mix

The provision of social and economic services involves the state, the market, the intermediate sector, also known as the non-profit sector, and the informal sector.

Table 2.1 Regional Governance Check, Quelle: Rakebrandt 2006 (Criteria are from Benz, 2004 and Fürst, 2004.)

	Initial situation	Yes	Unclear	No
A	There is a deficit in the region, which is also felt by society as such.			
B	The deficit is not a single problem, but a problem area.			
C	To work on the problem, there is a regionally assembled group.			
D	The group is unincorporated, which means that its assembly is not based on a previously made political (will) decision.			
E	Members of the group belong to the regional administration (employees, representatives, district).			
F	Members of the group belong to different local administrations (employees, municipalities).			
G	Members of the group belong to economic organizations with a direct connection to the region.			
H	Members of the group belong to social organizations of the region.			
I	Members join the group out of interest in the topic.			
J	Members of the group are personally affected by the problem.			
K	Members of the group are actively or passively "causing" the problem because of which the group is formed.			
L	The composition of the group has a balanced ratio of representative groups (D-J).			
M	There is agreement among members about a common regional connection.			
N	There are no status-related hierarchical structures.			
O	There is no pre-determined code of conduct for the session.			
P	The group is solution-oriented, but open to results.			
Q	Problem-solving happens through arguing and negotiating.			
R	The group is basically willing to learn.			
S	The members cooperate with each other voluntarily.			
T	There is no obligation to vote in accordance with a party or faction policy whatsoever.			
U	Members can withdraw from cooperation at any time.			

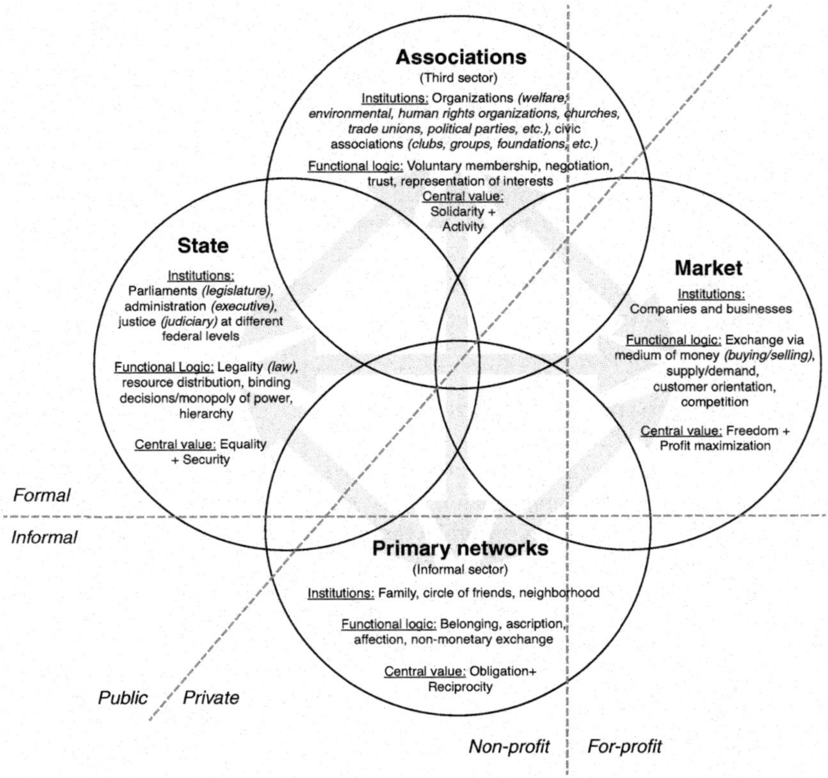

Fig. 2.5 Sectors of welfare production (Roß, 2018, p. 727)

The central actor in the state is the public administration, in the market it is companies, in the intermediate sector it is clubs, associations and foundations, and in the informal sector it is families and communities (Fig. 2.5). All sectors have different means of coordination. State structures are coordinated by law and hierarchy and the market by money and competition, while the intermediate sector is coordinated by communication and voluntariness, and the informal sector by personal relationships and obligations (cf. Evers & Olk, 1996). The individual sectors work together in a complex arrangement and are interwoven with each other. (Other perspectives are explained in detail in Chap. 3).

In the last two decades, institutional governance aspects in the social economy have been strongly associated with the guiding principle of the activating welfare state. The state increasingly withdrew to its guarantee function, private commercial providers, voluntary civic engagement and the informal sector were included, e.g., the involvement of family members was promoted. Regulatory measures were to be replaced by cooperative-oriented steering, dirigiste decisions by moderation of change processes, ordoliberal individual regulations by an orientation towards basic values, and the expansion of state influence areas by self-limitation to priorities.

The guiding principle of the activating state leads to a change in the role of institutions, as shown in the diagram (Fig. 2.6):

2.2.2 Governance and Administration

For Jann/Wegrich, what is special about the use of the concept of governance in the context of public administration is that trends regarding the role of public administration are analytically recorded and described, and requirements for as well as approaches to a reform of administration are justified and underpinned by theoretical concepts (Jann & Wegrich, 2010, p. 175).

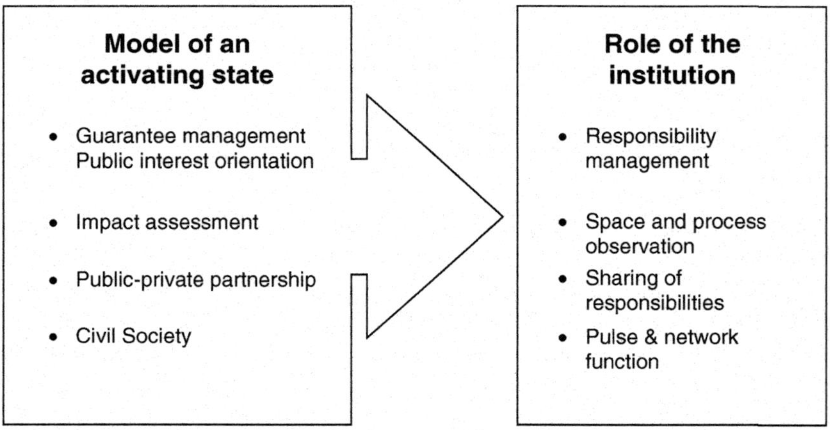

Fig. 2.6 Guiding principle of the activating state and role of institutions http://slideplayer.org/slide/1279610/. Accessed: 10.9.2021

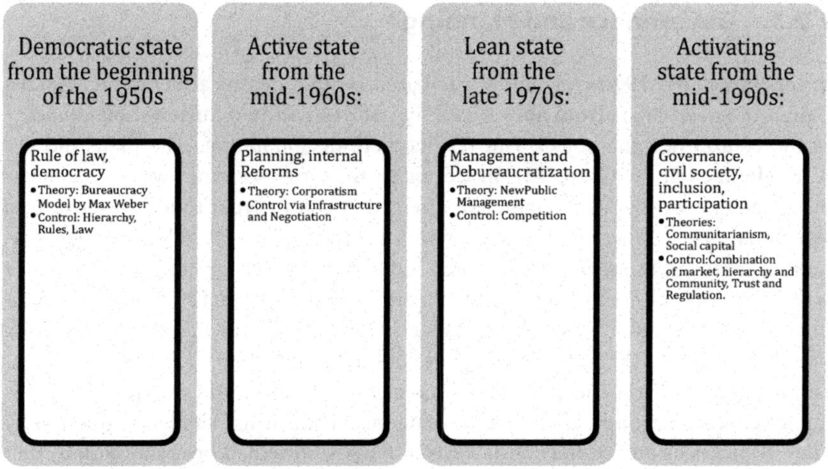

Fig. 2.7 Changes in the guiding principles of public administration (based on Jann & Wegrich, 2010, p. 177)

They point to changes in the guiding principles of public administration, as outlined in the following figure (2.7):

For Jann/Wegrich, governance is a new reform concept of administrative policy and is to be understood in contrast to the model of New Public Management. The New Public Management approach is efficiency-oriented. It is about customer orientation and quality. The central credo of New Public Management was that classical bureaucratic control leads to dysfunctional consequences at an early stage and therefore the concept of modern business management should be transferred and applied to public administration (Jann & Wegrich, 2010, p. 183). This concept included motivation instead of alimentation (performance-related pay), self-responsibility instead of hierarchy (decentralized resource responsibility), results instead of rules (contract management, product orientation) and cost accounting instead of cameralism (Jann & Wegrich, 2010, p. 183). Nevertheless, what was promised could only be partially redeemed, in part because management concepts were often transformed into bureaucratic structures by the bureaucracy itself.

The governance approach has a different context. It is participation-oriented. It is about civic engagement and about involving, activating and no longer steering and supplying social actors from above–"top down" (Jann & Wegrich, 2010, p. 184). This also has an impact on state regulatory approaches.

2.2.3 Governance and Planning

In the 1960s and 1970s, planning was based on the idea of a hierarchical-statist design of social areas from above, i.e., by politics with a ministerial bureaucracy as the central design subject. But results were disappointing. The plans did not work (Benz et al., 2007, p. 12). In Germany, the term 'steering' was used. Steering is understood to mean a targeted, directed action in order to no longer reform functional areas. Since the steering approach favors large actors such as associations, parties, administrations, etc., and individual citizens are rather a hindrance when considering controllability, the steering approach quickly reached its limits (Benz et al., 2007, 12 f.). Governance is the opposite of hierarchical steering (Mayntz, 2010, p. 38) and goes in the direction of delegation of former state regulations to the self-organization area of society and organizations. An example is higher education policy, in which the state has changed its detailed regulation by laws, ordinances and decrees in favor of a purpose-oriented programming of universities by target agreements.

2.3 Meta-level and Fundamentals of Good Governance

In third approximation, the principles of good governance are elaborated in terms of a metaperspective.

The World Bank's Africa study of 1989 is considered the beginning of the good governance debate. It comes to the conclusion that development aid fails in its intention if it is not managed and controlled within the framework of well-functioning public institutions (Czada, 2010, p. 201). Development aid funds were wasted because the necessary governance institutions were not taken into account (Czada, 2010, p. 203). In reaction, criteria for "good governance" were developed. These include the efficient design of public administration, the involvement of relevant social groups and minorities in decision-making, the containment of corruption and nepotism, and the establishment of rule of law and transparent relationships between public and private sector (Springer Gabler Verlag (ed.), Gabler Economic Dictionary, Keyword: Good Governance, online: 35/Archiv/127685/good-governance-v4.html).

Principles of good governance also came to be demanded in developed industrial countries, such as in the OECD's governance principles (1995):

- respect for the rule of law,
- openness, transparency and accountability to democratic institutions,
- fairness and equity in dealings with citizens, including mechanisms for consultation and participation,
- efficient, effective services,
- clear, transparent and applicable laws and regulations,
- consistency and coherence in policy formation,
- and high standards of ethical behaviour.

(Source: http://www.olev.de/g/good_gov.htm)

or in the five principles of "good governance" of the EU Commission:

- **Openness.** The organs should work more openly and, together with the Member States, explain what the EU does and how decisions are made. They should use a language that everyone can understand. Openness is so important because it can help to trust in complex institutions.
- **Participation.** How good, appropriate and effective EU policy is depends on the extent to which the actors are involved in the policy-making process—from conception to implementation. Increased participation leads to greater trust in the outcome as well as the policy of the institutions. The involvement's extent depends crucially on whether the central government levels of the Member States proceed with their policy development and implementation according to an "inclusive" concept.
- **Responsibility.** The distribution of roles in legislation and implementation must be clearer. Each EU institution must explain to citizens what it does in Europe and take responsibility for it. This greater clarity and accountability also applies to the Member States and all those who, at whatever level, contribute to the development and implementation of EU policy.
- **Effectiveness.** EU policy must be effective, timely and provide what is necessary, based on clear objectives, impact assessments and, where appropriate, experience. Effectiveness is also determined by whether the policy is implemented in a way that is appropriate in relation to its objectives, and whether the decisions are taken at the appropriate level.
- **Coherence.** Politics and concrete action must be coherent and easily comprehensible. The need for coherence in the Union is growing: more and more tasks have to be performed. The eastward enlargement will increase the

> EU's diversity even further. Challenges such as climate change and population development do not stop at the borders of the sectoral policies on which the Union is based. Regional and local bodies are increasingly involved in the EU's policy-making. Coherence requires political leadership and strong responsibility of the organs, so that a consistent approach can be taken within the complex system." (EU Commission, White Paper, 2001, 13 et seq.)

The principles of good governance correspond to the requirements of a complex society, and also offer a normative framework for the social economy, which is further developed on the meso level of "cooperation", which leads to the next chapter.

2.4 Control questions for Chap. 2

2.1 What is meant by "First Order Governance"?
2.2 Explain "Local Governance" with an example.
2.3 What is meant by "regional governance"?
2.4 What is meant by "Second Order Governance"?
2.5 What do you understand by "welfare mix"?
2.6 What characterizes the "activating welfare state"?
2.7 Which changes in public administration can be observed?
2.8 How can governance be distinguished from New Public Management?
2.9 What is the significance of governance in the field of state planning?
2.10 What is meant by "Third Order Governance"?
2.11 What are the origins of the "Good Governance Approach"?
2.12 How can "Good Governance" be guaranteed?

References

Arnig, N. (21. Januar 2008). Im Namen des Bürgers. *Frankfurter Rundschau.*

Benz, A. (Hrsg.). (2004). *Governance – Regieren in komplexen Regelsystemen* (1. Aufl.). VS Verlag.

Benz, A., Lütz, S., Schimank, U., & Simonis, G. (Hrsg.). (2007). *Handbuch Governance.* VS Verlag.

Bougmil, J., & Holtkamp, L. (2004). Local Governance und gesellschaftliche Integration. In S. Lange & U. Schimank (Hrsg.), *Governance und gesellschaftliche Integration* (S. 147–166). VS Verlag.

Bundesinstitut für Bau-, Stadt- und Raumforschung (BBSR) im Bundesamt für Bauwesen und Raumordnung (BBR) (Hrsg.). (2020). *Studie Lokale Ökonomie BIWAQ. ESF-Bundesprogramm „Bildung, Wirtschaft, Arbeit im Quartier – BIWAQ" – Projektabschlussbericht. Bonn.*

Bundesministerium des Innern, für Bau und Heimat (BMI). (2019). 20 Jahre integrierte Quartiersentwicklung. Die Soziale Stadt. https://www.bmi.bund.de/SharedDocs/downloads/DE/publikationen/themen/bauen/wohnen/20-jahre-soziale-stadt.pdf?__blob=publicationFile&v=3. Zugegriffen: 10. Sept. 2021.

Bundesministerium des Innern, für Bau und Heimat (BMI). (2021). Soziale Stadt, www.staedtebaufoerderung.info/StBauF/DE/Programm/SozialeStadt/soziale_stadt_node.html. Zugegriffen: 10. Sept. 2021.

Bundesministerium des Innern, für Bau und Heimat (BMI). (2019). Soziale Stadt. Das Programm der Städtebauförderung für benachteiligte Stadt- und Ortsteile, www.sozialestadt.de.

Czada, R. (2010). Good Governance als Leitkonzept für Regierungshandeln: Grundlagen, Anwendungen, Kritik. In A. Benz & N. Dose (Hrsg.), *Governance – Regieren in komplexen Regelsystemen.* (2., aktualisierte und veränderte Aufl.). VS Verlag.

Europäische Kommission. (2001). *Europäisches Regieren.* Weißbuch, Amt für amtliche Veröffentlichungen der Europäischen Gemeinschaften.

Evers, A., & Olk, T. (1996). Wohlfahrtspluralismus. Analytische und normativ-politische Dimensionen eines Leitbegriffs. In A. Evers & T. Olk (Hrsg.), *Wohlfahrtspluralismus. Vom Wohlfahrtsstaat zur Wohlfahrtsgesellschaft* (S. 9–62). Westdeutscher Verlag.

Fürst, D. (2007). Regional Governance. In A. Benz, S. Lütz, U. Schimank, & G. Simonis (Hrsg.), *Handbuch Governance* (S. 353–650). VS Verlag.

Fürst, D. (2004). Regional Governance. In A. Benz (Hrsg.), *Governance – Regieren in komplexen Regelsystemen* (1. Aufl., S. 45–64). VS Verlag.

Greca, R. (2005). Lokale Governance im Zeitalter der Globalisierung – ein neuer Mythos? In L. Kolhoff, R. Beck, H. D. Engelhardt, M. Hege, & J. Sandmann (Hrsg.), *Zwischen Ökonomie und sozialer Verantwortung* (S. 50–82). Ziel.

Häußermann, H., & Walther, U.-J. (2018). Soziale Stadt. In ARL – Akademie für Raumforschung und Landesplanung (Hrsg.), *Handwörterbuch der Stadt- und Raumentwicklung* (S. 2197–2206). ARL – Akademie für Raumforschung und Landesplanung, ISBN 978-3-88838-559-9, http://nbn-resolving.de/urn:nbn:de:0156-55992035. Zugegriffen: 10. Sept. 2021.

Jann, W., & Wegrich, K. (2010). Governance und Verwaltungspolitik: Leitbilder und Reformkonzepte. In A. Benz & N. Dose (Hrsg.), *Governance – Regieren in komplexen Regelsystemen* (2., aktualisierte und veränderte Aufl., S. 175–200). VS Verlag.

Kooiman, J. (2003). *Governing as Governance.* Sage Publications Ltd.

Mayntz, R. (2010). Governance im modernen Staat. In A. Benz & N. Dose (Hrsg.), *Governance – Regieren in komplexen Regelsystemen* (2., aktualisierte und veränderte Aufl., S. 37–48). VS Verlag.

Rakebrandt, D. (2006). Regional Governance in der Jugendarbeit dargestellt am Beispiel der Region Verden, nicht veröffentlichte Masterarbeit an der FH Braunschweig/Wolfenbüttel. *Masterstudiengang Sozialmanagement.*

Roß, P. S. (2018). Governance. In K. Grunwald & A. Langer (Hrsg.), *Sozialwirtschaft. Handbuch für Wissenschaft und Praxis* (S. 726–738). Nomos.

Meso Level: "Cooperation" 3

Abstract

After considering the interface of state and society at the macro level, the focus is now on social businesses and their relationships with the environment at the meso level. Governance structures are located in the context of the corporate governance discussion as far as the internal relationship is concerned, and in the course of networks and cooperation, as far as the external relationship is concerned.

Learning Objectives
In the following chapter, you will learn, based on the model of the principal-agent conflict, about corporate governance structures within the internal relationship and structures of cooperation in socio-spatial networks within the external relationship of social businesses. It will be shown that adequate structures must be created in order to enable cooperation.

3.1 Within the Internal Relationship: Corporate Governance

Corporate governance is about the "structures, rules and practices of the control and supervision of companies" (Eberle, 2010, p. 155). This approach originated in Great Britain in the 1990s, where there was a wave of corporate bankruptcies attributed to principal-agent conflicts, i.e., conflicts of interest between managers (agents) and owners (principals), as well as lack of supervision. Since ownership

L. Kolhoff, *Governance in the Social Economy*,
https://doi.org/10.1007/978-3-658-38743-3_3

and control diverge in many companies, the governance problem is as follows: How can the owners of the company (principals) prevent managers (agents) from pursuing their own interests instead of the interests of the owners (principals)?

In Germany, corporate governance became a current topic in the 2000s through the establishment of the Corporate Governance Commission. The German Corporate Governance Code, which was adopted in 2002, is intended to increase confidence in management at publicly traded companies. Issues include the role and function of the board of directors, the role and function of the supervisory board, the interaction between the board of directors and the supervisory board, transparency, accounting and auditing regulations. While the corporate governance debate in Anglo-Saxon countries focuses on the conflict of interest between managers (agents) and owners (principals) and thus seeks mechanisms able to ensure that companies are run in the interest of shareholders, the German debate is extended to stakeholders such as employees. Examples include committees such as supervisory boards of large companies in which trade unions are represented.

VW Diesel Scandal

Despite these regulations, however, there are limits to best practices in corporate governance, as shown by the VW diesel scandal. "This giant corporation is a textbook example of a completely person- or owner-focused monocratic leadership style, the functioning of which is based solely on the power of a few" (Handelsblatt, October 13, 2015).

The corporate governance debate also extends to the non-profit sector. For example, the Corporate Governance Commission is of the opinion that "there is a need for discussion, especially with regard to such associations which claim tax privileges, collect donations or operate as ideal associations within the so-called ancillary purpose privilege as commercial enterprises" (Baums, 2001, p. 6).

There are principal-agent conflicts in non-profit organizations. For example, in the case of an association, the members and the board of directors can be seen as principals and the management as an agent. Accordingly, their interests differ and are often not made visible by the structures used (Beck, 2010), because in many associations honorary board members do both—management and supervision—thereby creating a situation adverse to effective economic supervision (Bangert, 2010, p. 208). Therefore, the point is to clarify roles and install a supervisory board in addition to the board of directors or management that is able to exercise effective economic supervision and control (Bachert, 2006, p. 15).

Schuhen formulates 5 areas of requirements for supervisory boards:

1. Independence, autonomy and transparency. He calls for a dual management system, that is, a separation of operational management, board of directors, management and supervision. The supervisory function is to be carried out voluntarily with appropriate compensation. The supervisory board ensures the necessary transparency, monitors compliance with the articles of association, compliance with statutory social norms, etc.
2. Cooperation with the operational management. The strategic orientation is coordinated between supervisory board and management. The supervisory board regulates contractual matters of the operational management and is responsible for its job description.
3. Size, representation and diversity. The supervisory body should consist of at least two or, better still, more individuals. Members should have multi-professional qualifications. Relatives of affected people can only become members if there is no direct conflict of interest. Members should be able to represent groups of claimants in the manner of a social advocacy role. The group should be composed heterogeneously in terms of age and gender.
4. Self-organization, self-monitoring and necessary resources. Regular meetings at least twice a year and time slots for strategic planning are required. The supervisory board should be time-limited with the possibility of re-election.
5. Use of suitable instruments of supervision. There should be suitable instruments (risk management, quality management and key performance indicators, etc.). (Schuhen, 2014, 525 f.)

A key feature of corporate governance is the supervisory board's independence. Exclusion criteria for membership on a supervisory board would be:

- member of the executive board or management,
- family relationships with members of the executive board or management,
- individuals employed by the auditor,
- individuals in a competitive relationship with the provider.

People affected who are in a business relationship with the provider should only be included if there is no conflict of interest (Bangert, 2010, p. 208).

In addition to the requirements for supervision and management, the special features of social institutions must also be taken into account, as shown by the example of integration assistance:

- Special features are the cooperation of voluntary and professional managers,
- the involvement of people with (intellectual) disabilities,
- with parents and other relatives in decision-making bodies,
- the principle of free voluntary work,
- the membership of employees in the association,
- the roles of parents as employers and customers, etc. (Auer, 2010, p. 211)

The Lebenshilfe Corporate Governance Code takes these special features into account.

Lebenshilfe's Corporate Governance Code

Regardless of the legal form of Lebenshilfe as a non-profit association or as a company under private law, there will usually be a full-time management. It is appointed by the board and takes on tasks for the association. The association's board is its governing body and supervises the management. It must therefore be examined whether, in addition to the general meeting, there should be a supervisory board elected or appointed by it, which exercises the supervisory function over a board that, according to the articles of association or club law, manages the affairs of the association. This committee can monitor the board more intensively than the general meeting and meet more frequently.

2.1 Tasks and responsibilities of the general meeting and the supervisory board

2.1.1 The general meeting takes on the tasks specified in the articles of association.

2.1.2 It supervises the management bodies (voluntary board, possibly full-time management) or appoints a supervisory board for this purpose.

2.1.3 It decides on all basic and guiding measures that are not assigned to a supervisory board or the management bodies.

2.2 Tasks and responsibilities of the board and management as well as their cooperation with the general meeting and the supervisory board

2.2.1 Supervisory board, association board and management work closely together for the benefit of the association. They are obliged to further its interests.

2.2.2 The board is responsible for the strategic orientation of the association. It works closely with the management and the supervisory board.

2.2.3 The board is also responsible for the management of business, which can be delegated to a full-time management. This configuration is the basis for the following remarks.

2.2.4 This management is then responsible for the management of the association's current affairs with all its facilities and services.

2.2.5 The composition, tasks and responsibilities, powers, information and reporting obligations of the supervisory board, the board and the management are to be regulated by business regulations, unless stipulated in the articles of association.

2.2.6 All levels observe the rules of proper corporate or association management as well as delegation and control and exercise their office with due care.

2.2.7 Good association management requires an open and constructive exchange of the supervisory and management bodies. Comprehensive confidentiality of the members of the supervisory and management bodies as well as a guarantee of the secrecy of individuals involved by the supervisory board, the board and the management are of great importance for this. This also applies to an appreciative, respectful coexistence of honorary and full-time officials in the committees. The appreciation of honorary and civic engagement is a matter of course.

2.2.8 People with disabilities as well as parents and relatives are members of the supervisory and management bodies and receive the support necessary to perform their tasks.

2.2.9 Sufficient insurance of all members of the committees is to be provided.

2.3 Board

2.3.1 In assembling the board, it is desirable that members have as many different qualifications as possible and are able to meet the content and time requirements of board work. The key points of the search committee, which are printed in the appendix, provide guidance. In accordance with the history and identity of Lebenshilfe as a parent and self-help association, it is important to have an effective representation of these groups in the board's composition.

2.3.2 Boards in Lebenshilfe have a demanding task, must be suited for this and are informed and qualified accordingly.

2.3.3 Honorary members of the board do not receive any remuneration for their work. They are entitled to reimbursement of their expenses. In the case of lump sum expense allowances, transparency and a corresponding resolution by the general meeting are mandatory.

2.3.4 If members of staff of Lebenshilfe are also members of the association, the rules governing any restrictions that may apply to the exercise of the active right to vote must be laid down in the Articles of Association. A possibility of exercising the passive right to vote is not recommended because of possible conflicts of interest.

2.3.5 Board members must not, in connection with their work, demand, promise or accept any benefits or other advantages for themselves or for any other person from any third party, or grant any unjustified advantages to any third party.

2.3.6 Board members must avoid conflicts of interest. If they nevertheless exist, they must be disclosed to the board and to supervisory bodies. This is particularly true in the case of conflicts of interest in relations involving financial flows or special dependencies: with customers and clients, with suppliers and business partners, grantors and donors, payers, regulatory authorities and in employment and care relationships.

2.3.7 The introduction of members to the work of the board of directors is a necessary activity of the incumbent Board of Directors.

2.4 Management and employees

2.4.1 The activity of management is regulated by the board of directors in a job description and/or rules of procedure.

2.4.2 Full-time managers receive a remuneration for their activity in Lebenshilfe organization which is appropriate to the scope of duties and responsibility, the size of the company, the entrepreneurial risk and the liability, and which takes into account increased workplace risk in the case of managing directors of a GmbH.

2.4.3 The exercise of paid and unpaid secondary activities and a competition ban for members of the management have to be regulated.

2.4.4 With regard to exemption from the restrictions of § 181 BGB (prohibition of self-contracting, in-house transactions), regulations are to be made—taking into account any requirements of donors, if necessary.

2.4.5 Management and employees must avoid conflicts of interest. If they nevertheless exist, they have to be disclosed to superiors or supervisory bodies. This applies in particular to conflicts of interest in relations which are linked with financial flows or dependencies: with customers and clients, with suppliers and business partners, credit and grant donors, service providers, supervisory authorities as well as in employment and care relationships.

2.4.6 Members of management and employees may neither demand, promise or accept benefits or other advantages for themselves or for other individuals from third parties in connection with their activity, nor grant unjustified advantages to third parties.

2.5 Leadership and Monitoring

2.5.1 Associations are obliged to have a meaningful accounting system, transparent financial management, functioning control and audit mechanisms and overall sustainable economic and ethical corporate conduct. This is to be done in proportion to their sales and investment volumes.

2.5.2 Control and supervision serve Lebenshilfe associations to ensure compliance with their principles and the achievement of their ideal, material and financial goals. In order to control and monitor, they should create clear structures and processes and take measures in a planned and sustainable manner. The regular, planned collection of corresponding indices and data is the basis for steering, controlling the achievement of goals and, if necessary, taking corrective action.

2.5.3 The association should have a reporting and documentation system which defines all relevant information and communication channels as well as reporting obligations. This enables supervisory and management bodies to exercise their supervisory, management and decision-making functions comprehensively and appropriately.

2.5.4 The statutory and regulatory requirements and regulations on public benefit and fundraising as well as the provisions of the donors on the use and evidence of the use of funds made available are complied with.

2.5.5 The Lebenshilfe organisation should install a risk management system (risk analysis, risk management, risk control) appropriate to the scope of its business in order to increase transparency of existing risks and to recognise potential existential risks at an early stage.

2.5.6 Lebenshilfe deals with a variety of target groups, the most important ones of which are people with disabilities, parents and relatives as well as members of the association. In the association's reporting, specific needs of these individual groups must be taken into account in terms of content and presentation.

2.5.7 Lebenshilfe deals openly and constructively with complaints from members, parents, people with disabilities, employees and customers. Regulations for complaint management are set jointly by board and management

2.6 Accounting and audits

2.6.1 The association creates a proper annual financial statement.

2.6.2 The association should prepare a financial statement. This, as well as the integrity of the financial and business management, may be subject of an audit by the independent auditor.

2.6.3 The supervisory board or the board of directors decide on the commissioning of an independent auditor and on the scope of the audit, priorities or special audit items. The auditor reports to the board of directors and the supervisory board the main results of the audit as well as any special incidents.

2.6.4 The association should explain to the general assembly whether and to what extent it applies the Corporate Governance Code and, in the event of deviations from the provisions of the Code, justify these.

(Source: Corporate Governance Code Good Corporate Governance in the Social Welfare. A recommendation of the Federal Association of Social Welfare for people with intellectual disabilities e.V. for their member organizations, Status: Summer 2012, Source: https://lebenshilfe-rlp.de/pdf/archiv/02_2012_01_Corporate_Governance_Kodex.pdf.)

In the non-profit sector, maximizing profits is not the primary focus, even though competition has increased and economic aspects are gaining more and more importance. It is not the shareholders, but the contributors and taxpayers who bear the entrepreneurial risk. Thus, principal-agent conflicts in the non-profit sector differ from those in the commercial sector and, in addition to the interests of internal stakeholders, those of external ones, such as clients, relatives, investors, cost bearers, donors, actors in the political environment, other carriers, partner companies and supervisory authorities, must also be taken into account (Bangert, 2010, p. 207). The task of corporate governance in NPOs is to ensure that the goals of the organization's most important stakeholders are represented (Siebart, 2006, p. 243). Therefore, it is of great importance to be able to assess the relevant stakeholders. Depending on the scope of influence as well as its importance for the company's conduct, their influence can be categorized and evaluated on the basis of the criteria of power, urgency and legitimacy, according to Mitchell, Agle and Wood (1997, in Theuvsen, 2001, p. 10). If stakeholders possess power, they can assert themselves well in situations characterized by conflicting interests (Theuvsen, 2001, p. 7 et seq.). Actions that are considered appropriate within a social system are considered legitimate and can thus be assigned to the area of legitimacy. Demands of stakeholders gain urgency when corporate governance has to deal with them. In contrast, demands of stakeholders who are powerless to influence processes are bound to be ignored (Theuvsen, 2001, p. 11).

7 types are distinguished depending on the combination of the criteria:

Resting Stakeholders:	They have power, do not bring urgent claims and would not be legitimate to do so.
Negligible Stakeholders:	They are legitimate, but have neither power nor urgent concerns.
Demanding Stakeholders:	They loudly present their concerns, but are neither legitimate nor have the power to enforce their interests.
Dominant Stakeholders:	They have power and legitimacy, but see no reason to present their concerns as long as "business as usual" (Theuvsen, 2001, p. 11) prevails.
Dangerous Stakeholders:	They pursue their own interests vigorously and have the power to enforce them.
Dependent Stakeholders:	They bring legitimate and urgent demands forward, but do not have the power to impose their concerns against the will of others.
Definitive Stakeholders:	They have the power to impose their legitimate interests. Their concerns are of high urgency.

Traffic light colors are supposed to signal the importance of stakeholders (Fig. 3.1).

This stakeholder analysis is a snapshot and stakeholders can assume different roles over time. Therefore, regular stakeholder analysis is helpful to recognize and consider different expectations.

In order to be able to involve all relevant stakeholders, social-economic organizations, in their external relations, must act within the social space of governance structures networked with state, economic, associative and informal actors.

3.2 Within External Relations: Networks and Cooperation in the Social Environment

3.2.1 Networks

Networks in the sense of cooperative coordination can be considered a form of governance (Wald & Jansen, 2007).

Networks can be divided into natural and artificial networks or into primary, secondary and tertiary networks (Fig. 3.2) (Bullinger & Nowak, 1998).

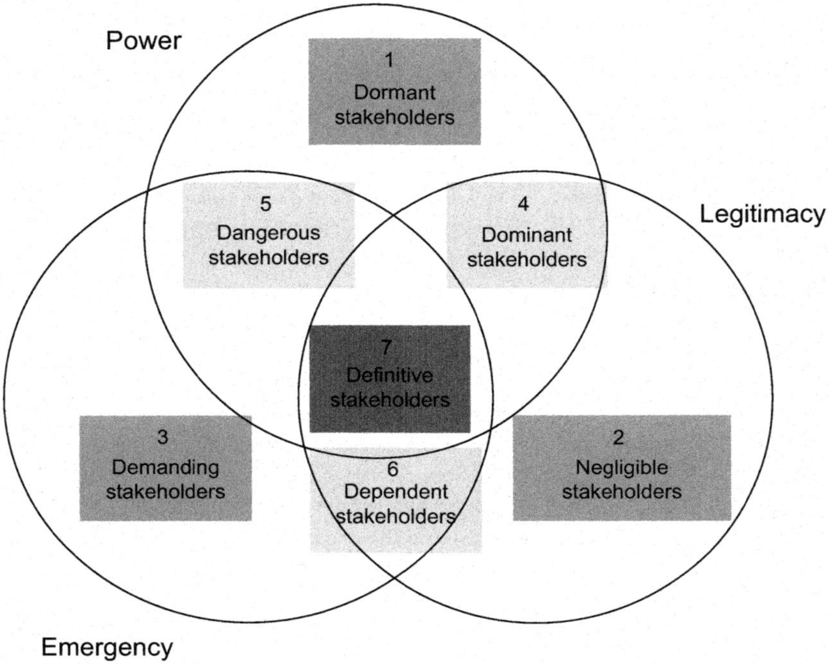

Fig. 3.1 Stakeholder typology (after Mitchell et al., 1997, in: Theuvsen, 2001, p. 10)

You either choose or are born into primary networks. They are about personal relationships between people and other people. Examples are families, friendships or neighborhoods. You are socialized in secondary networks. Examples are kindergartens, schools, universities, etc., but also self-help groups and community centers. Primary and secondary networks belong to the natural networks. They promote social relationships and social capital at the individual level and work according to the principle of exchanging services. The tertiary networks are artificial networks equipped with professional resources. These are collaborations that are characterized by inter-institutional relationships.

To analyze networks, it is, in a first step, necessary to identify the most important actors (carriers, contacts, offers and possible cooperation) and, in a second step, to analyze the relationships between the actors, as shown in an example

Primary networks	are not organized (e.g., family, relatives, friends, close private collegial relations)
Secondary networks	are either weakly organized (self-help circles, neighborhood centers) or strongly organized like associations and organizations. Primary and secondary networks belong to the natural networks.
Tertiary networks	are artificial networks. This includes the non-profit third sector, and it includes the markets. (Industry, trade, etc.)

Fig. 3.2 Networks (Florian, 2008, p. 37)

from the Braunschweig project "Stadtteil in der Schule" (Kolhoff & Gebhardt, 2016) (Figs. 3.3 and 3.4).

1. Central actors in the social environment of the Altmühlstraße primary school
2. Representation of networking

Networks should not only be visualized, but also analyzed more deeply. The approach by Vester is helpful in this endeavor (Vester, 1993).

Assignment 3.1:

1. Take a large poster and all necessary materials.
2. Phrase your problem as a question or thesis. Write this as headline on the poster.
3. Determine (possibly on cards, first) a series of elements (sizes, factors, areas, variables) that play a role within your problem. Think also of factors that are often not considered in relation to this problem (e.g., technical factors in social problems, human factors in technical problems, etc.). If you have found many factors more than can be processed in the given time, select the ones that seem most important to you.

4. On the left side of your poster, write the determined elements in circles that are arranged in no particular order in a field (Fig. 3.5).
5. For each element, check if it influences any other element in any way. For each influence found, draw an arrow from the influencing element to the influenced one. (Do not use a double arrow if there is influence on both sides.)

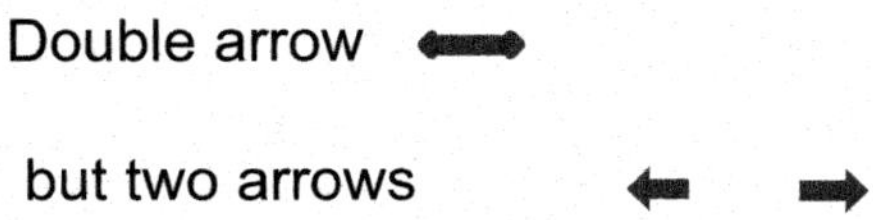

	Actor
	Schools:
	Primary school Altmühlstraße
1	Secondary School LifeLearning
2	Primary school Ilmenaustraße
3	Free Waldorf School
	Daycare centers:
4	Ev. KITA Noah's Ark
5	Ev. KITA Mittenmark
6	**Caritas Day Care Center St. Maximilian Kolbe**
7	**AWO Children's and Family Centre Muldeweg**
8	**AWO daycare center**
9	Walldorf Kindergarten
10	DRK crèche
11	Till makes Bimbambule
	Educational Provider:
12	Le@rn & Live Braunschweig-West e.V.
	Cultural and recreational facilities:
13	**Children and Teen Club White Rose**
14	Culture Point West (Community House)

Fig. 3.3 Central actors in the social space of the Altmühlstraße primary school (Marschik, 2016, 234 et seq.)

15	House of talents
	(Sports) clubs:
16	Coronary Sports Club Braunschweig eV
17	Rifle club Belfort 1896 e.V.
18	SC Victoria Braunschweig e.V.
19	HC Braunschweig e.V.
20	Allotment garden clubs
	Community centres
21	Venue Saalestr.
22	Meeting point Am Queckenberg
23	Meeting place
24	House of encounter
	Churches/faith communities:
25	Baptist congregation
26	Emmaus Parish
27	St. Cyriakus
	(Welfare) associations:
28	DRK
29	Knights of St. John
30	THW
	Housing associations:
31	Wiederaufbau eG
	Seniors (inpatient facilities):
32	Ambet
33	Muldeweg Senior Citizens' Centre
	Actors outside the social space:
A	BBG eG
B	Nibelungen Wohnbau GmbH
C	Caritas Association Braunschweig
D	Ev. day care centre Ahrplatz
E	AWO Brunswick
F	With Us Community
	Neighborhood-level networks:
I	Citizens' Association Weststadt e.V
II	Weststadtplenum for children and young people
III	AGeWe

Fig. 3.3 (continued)

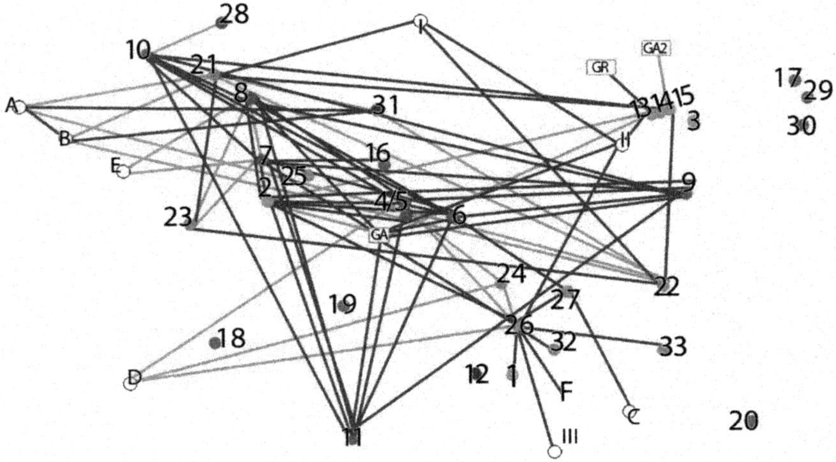

Fig. 3.4 Carrier structures, cooperation and networks—social space primary school Altmühlstraße (same carrier: red; cooperation/networking: blue) (Marschik, 2016, p. 56)

Fig. 3.5 Depiction of a network of elements

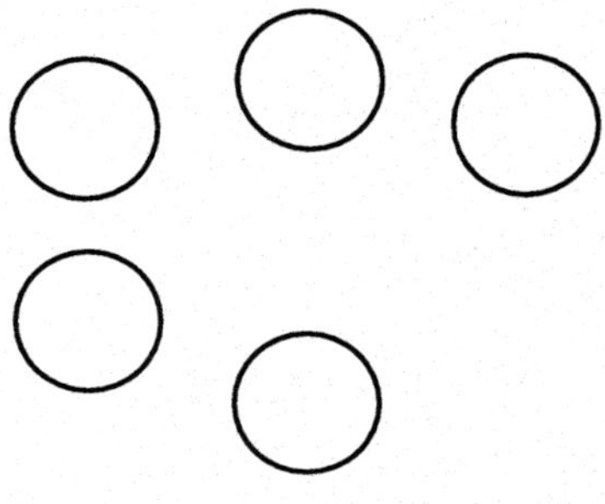

Now you have a hint as to whether your problem is a network (system), and, if so, you have a first overview of the networking and interactions of the problem areas.

6. Draw an evaluation scheme next to the network (see point 12). Use at least as many rows and columns (capital letters) as you have found elements.
7. Enter your elements, one below the other, in the "Effect of" column (far left) in any order (Vester, 1993, p. 143).

8. Now fill in all the empty boxes in the field framed by the capital letters by evaluating the individual interactions: Estimate how strongly each element affects the other elements. For this, enter the numbers 0 to 3.

- 0 = no influence
- 1 = weak influence
- 2 = moderate influence
- 3 = strong influence

9. Add the numbers in each row next to the element from left to right, and enter the sum in the AS column. This will give you the active sum of each element. All the numbers added from top to bottom under one letter give the passive sum (PS) of the element.
   "The element that most strongly influences the others (quite apart from how it is influenced itself) will then have the highest active sum. The element which is itself influenced the strongest will receive the highest passive sum" (Vester, 1993, 144 et seq.).
10. Divide the active sum of each element by its passive sum (AS: PS = Quotient Q).
    "The element with the highest Q-number is then the *active element*, the one with the lowest Q-number the *reactive element*" (Vester, 1993, p. 145).
    - **Active element** "influences all others the most, but is influenced by them the least" (Vester, 1993, p. 142).
    - **Passive element** "influences the others the least, but is influenced by them the most" (Vester, 1993, p. 142).
11. Multiply the active sum of each element by its passive sum and write the result in the P column (AS x PS = Product P).
    The element with the highest P number is the *critical element*, the one with the lowest P number *the resting (buffering) element.*
    - **Critical element** "influences the others most strongly and is influenced by them just as strongly" (Vester, 1993, p. 142).
    - **Resting or buffering element** "influences the others least and is influenced by them least" (Vester, 1993, p. 143).
12. Now use the results in both diagrams on your wall chart to highlight or label the four special elements.
    Evaluation scheme (Fig. 3.6)

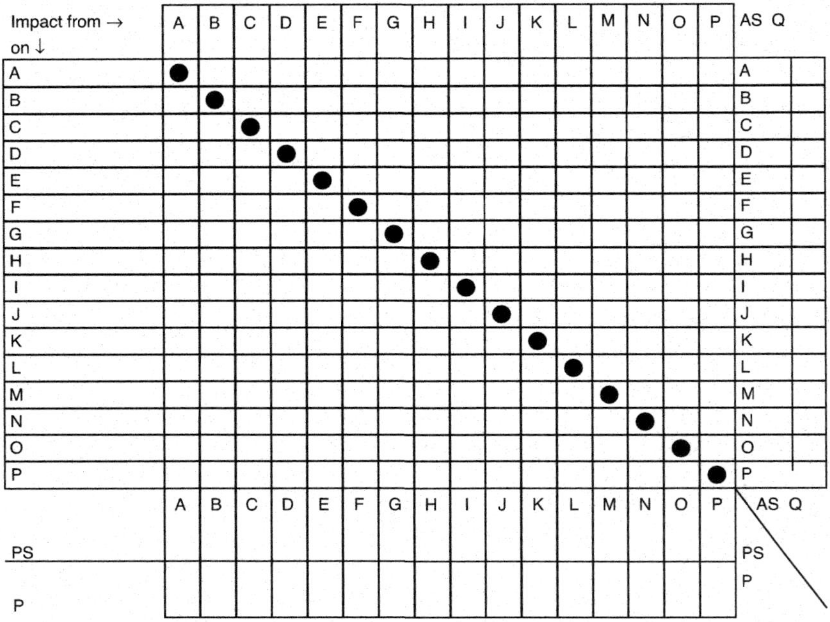

Fig. 3.6 Evaluation scheme

This analysis is followed by coordination and alignment with the network partners. It should be noted that networks must be coordinated in a different way to classical organizations (Schubert, 2008; Becker et al., 2011). While hierarchical government structures are long-term and characterized by the conflict regulation pattern of power, network-oriented forms of governance have a medium-term time horizon and are regulated by negotiations (Table 3.1). Their advantage lies in

Table 3.1 Typology of forms of coordination (Weyer, 2000, p. 7)

Coordination type	Market	Hierarchy/organization	Network
Coordination means	Prices	Formal rules	Trust
Coordination pattern	Spontaneous, specific	Regulated, unspecific	Discursive
Actor relations	Independent	Dependent	Interdependent
Access	Open	Regulated	Limited, exclusive
Time horizon	Short-term	Long-term	Medium-term
Conflict regulation	Law	Power	Negotiation

joint action, thereby incentivizing partners to cooperate and negotiate when conflicts arise, instead of trying to achieve their own goals at the expense of others. Networks' most important coordination tool is trust, their coordination pattern is discursive and access to them is limited and exclusive.

Common goals, values and experiences play a decisive role in networks, because networks are only viable under certain conditions. It should be noted that organizations are closed off from the environment and operate independently (Luhmann, 2004). Within networks, however, everything is about establishing points of contact and cooperating with the environment. This is possible if the participating systems have structural couplings, that is, if expectation structures are built in with which systems are sensitized to the codes of other systems. It must be checked whether organizations participating in a network have internal structures and operations at all suitable for cooperation with the environment.

Limits of Network Work

For example, building networks involving the judiciary is very difficult because the judiciary operates independently according to the code *right/wrong*. Therefore, cooperation with it is often rejected as interference with the legal system. Likewise, cooperation between social work and police is difficult. This is due to the fact that social work is characterized by the code *inclusion/exclusion* (Baecker, 1994) and considers everything from the perspective of inclusion[1], while the police are responsible for maintaining internal security. Maintaining internal security is the difference that distinguishes the police system from the environment, rendering the police a specific system. At the same time, the police observe the world on the basis of this difference. Accordingly, they only perceive and react to what is relevant to this difference. Attempts at cooperating quickly reach their limits. For example, the expectation of the police that youth welfare organizations should quickly contact juvenile offenders in order to restore law and order may reach its limits because youth welfare organizations take an inclusive approach when dealing with this problem area.

Cooperation between different social systems is only possible if they have internal structures and processes in place which make the operations of the other

[1] The aim is to integrate or reintegrate people into society.

system appear relevant to them. These internal structures need to be established in order to enable a structural coupling of the systems.

Such structural couplings, however, are often missing, making networks very dependent on people. Therefore, it should be checked whether decision-makers who are in a position to implement results in their organization or to initiate corresponding processes can be won over to networks in order to establish couplings. If, on the other hand, committed but poorly equipped representatives of the organization participate in these processes, there will be only little effect, unfortunately. Success therefore depends heavily on the actors' personal position within the respective organizations and institutions. Consequently, it is necessary to structurally involve the key decision-makers and to establish political and administrative security within networks of the social economy dependent on public decisions.

Political will to support network structures can be generated by scientific studies in which the need to support networking efforts is shown, as illustrated by the example of the network agency of the Berlin Stattbau GmbH.

Study by the German Institute for Urban Studies

The basis for the establishment of the agency was a study by the German Institute for Urban Studies (difu, 2007), which described the effects of demographic development, such as population decline and aging, on housing construction, social security systems and the labor market (difu, 2007, 16 et seq.). It also pointed out developments such as a population's heterogenization through migration, isolation of individuals through the dissolution of family ties and lifestyle changes (difu, 2007, 20 et seq.). From the interaction of demographic development and the housing market situation, the difu concluded that "above all, support for older people and households with children is required in order to realize their housing wishes" (difu, 2007, p. 33). Furthermore, the institute assumes that in future, more communal models of construction and housing will be created, because, among other things, family life forms are increasingly "replaced by the coexistence of people of different ages in 'elective affinities', which are mainly based on common interests and lifestyles" (difu, 2007, p. 34). It therefore promotes support of intergenerational social relationships, which also manifest themselves spatially in the form of communal housing and communal living. This support is to be provided by the Network Agency Generation Wohnen, which is charged with two tasks: Acting as a consulting center with regard to development and implementation of community-based intergenerational housing projects, and establishing connections to the housing industry. Its main task "aside from providing initial advice to interested parties and housing projects on a case-by-case basis" is "linking existing services and cooperation between the various levels of administration and public institutions" (difu, 2007, p. 7). The agency is supposed to win over both citizens and actors from the housing industry and municipal housing companies, housing associations and private homeowners as well as banks and mortgage lenders. In other words, its task is networking.

On the basis of the difu study, the Berlin Stattbau GmbH was commissioned, on 01.04.2008, to operate a network agency. To secure its work, an internal steering group comprising urban development, labor, social affairs, property fund, etc., was formed in order to coordinate the upcoming tasks. The network agency provides this group with information, it coordinates, moderates and keeps records.

Secured in this way, Stattbau can, in a third step, carry out the actual networking and support and accompany rental, developer or cooperative models for intergenerational living.

Stattbau is accompanied by employees of the network agency Generationen Wohnen, who are adept in techniques and methods of networking and are able to take into account the different codes of the parties involved. While, for example, the housing industry is pragmatically shaped by business economics, administration, social economy and interested parties each speak different languages. Here, it is necessary to translate and establish connections. Personal qualifications, such as the ability to work neutrally and in a task-oriented way, to back something, to avoid creating straw fires and to stay with an issue instead—these skills are just as important as authenticity and the ability to communicate and motivate.

Networking in the social economy is often structured by social space. How cooperation in social space can be structured will now be illustrated using municipal landscapes of education and participation as examples.

3.2.2 Municipal Landscapes of Education and Participation as Examples of Cooperation in Social Space

The term social space describes spatially delimited quarters (Riege & Schubert, 2019, 1 et seq.) on the one hand. On the other hand, social spaces can also be defined as resource spaces, with a focus on cooperation. An example of this are municipal landscapes of education and participation.

Municipal Educational Landscapes

In Germany, the demand for municipal educational landscapes is closely linked to the "PISA shock" caused by the results of the PISA (Programme for International Student Assessment) study of the OECD in 2001. The study showed, among other things, that the German education system relies heavily on the help of parents and that educational opportunities in Germany are unevenly distributed. As a result, a change of perspective was announced under the motto "Education is more than school—school is more than education" (Twelfth Children's & Youth Report, 2005, p. 12). Early childhood education and all-day schools were expanded and, based on an initiative of the German Association of Towns and Municipalities in 2007, municipal landscapes of education were introduced "in the sense of a networked system of education, training and care" (Aachen Declaration, 2007, p. 2).

"The main features of a local educational landscape are:

- Starting point for the organization of educational and learning processes are the individual's potential and its development throughout life. No child, no adolescent may be left behind.
- The actors responsible for education work together on the basis of binding structures: family, child and youth welfare, school, culture, sport, economy, etc.
- Parents or families are involved as central education partners.
- Transitions are made possible and designed according to the principle of 'connections instead of exclusions'.
- Cultural education is included as an important part of holistic education." (Aachen Declaration, 2007, p. 2)

Since education does not only take place in school and children as well as adolescents are educated in many places and on many occasions, the task of municipal educational landscapes is to connect different learning environments with each other and to link formal educational processes in formal settings (for example in schools) with informal educational processes (for example in youth centers) (Fig. 3.7). Instead of institutions, children and adolescents and their educational biographies are brought into focus in order to ensure that all children and adolescents "acquire a minimum of competences for shaping their own biography as a basis for maturity as well as willingness to perform and ability to perform" (Heinrich-Böll Foundation, 2011, p. 7).

Municipal Participation Landscapes

The term "municipal participation landscapes" is based on the concept of municipal educational landscapes. While the focus of municipal educational landscapes is on the interactions between formal education in schools and informal

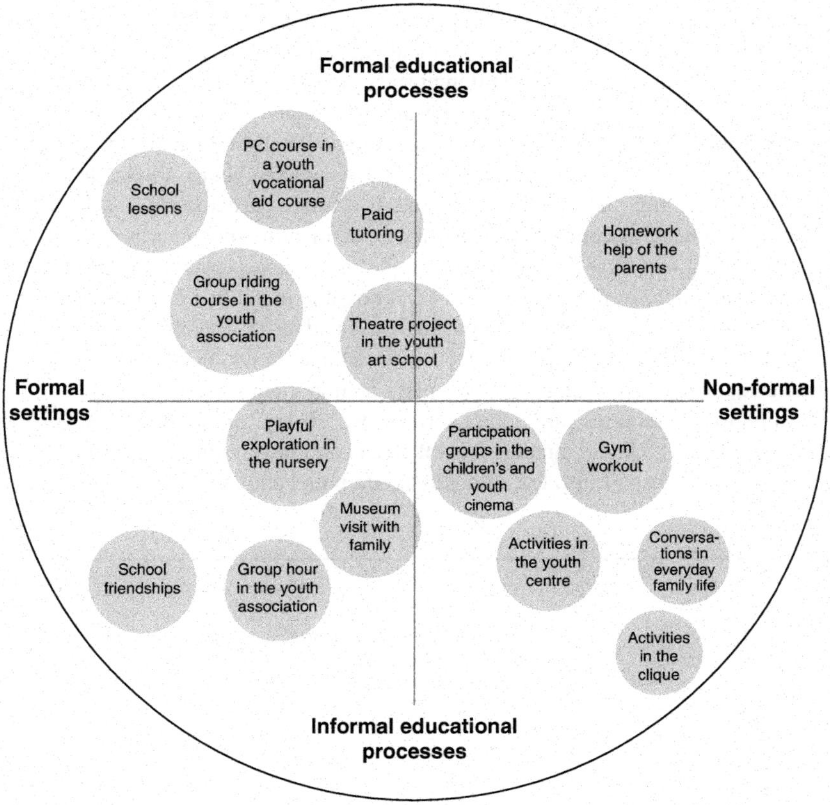

Fig. 3.7 Educational modalities (German Bundestag, 2005, p. 97)

educational processes in families as well as in child and youth services, municipal participation landscapes deal with the interplay of both formal support options offered by public and private providers and informal support in the social environment in order to promote participation. For this purpose, social resources must be activated and professional and non-professional support must be combined.

The basic principle of municipal participation landscapes is: "All stakeholders are to be included." In addition to formal organizations and institutions of care, assistance and participation, this also includes informal actors. In addition to formal processes, informal ones and, furthermore formal settings, non-formal ones are to be considered. People with disabilities are at the center of any municipal participation landscape. The focus is on individual support of every person with the goal of their successful participation. Different stages of development must be taken into account. In childhood, support regarding family care and socialization are of great importance, as is the networking of different offers for physiological care, mobility support or supported communication. For adolescents and young adults, the aspect of formal schooling plays a significant role. It is about participation in school and vocational education coupled with participation in different opportunities in the social environment. For adult disabled people, municipal participation landscapes support the search for or creation of work, if possible in the first labor market. Furthermore, it is necessary to satisfy housing needs and create meaningful daily structures, but also to ensure care and support. In old age, in addition to creating daily structures, the issue of care and support plays an important role.

Municipal structures are characterized by strong pillarization (Schubert, 2018a) (Fig. 3.8). On the municipal level, social and health offices are responsible for people with disabilities. For disabled children and adolescents, there are youth

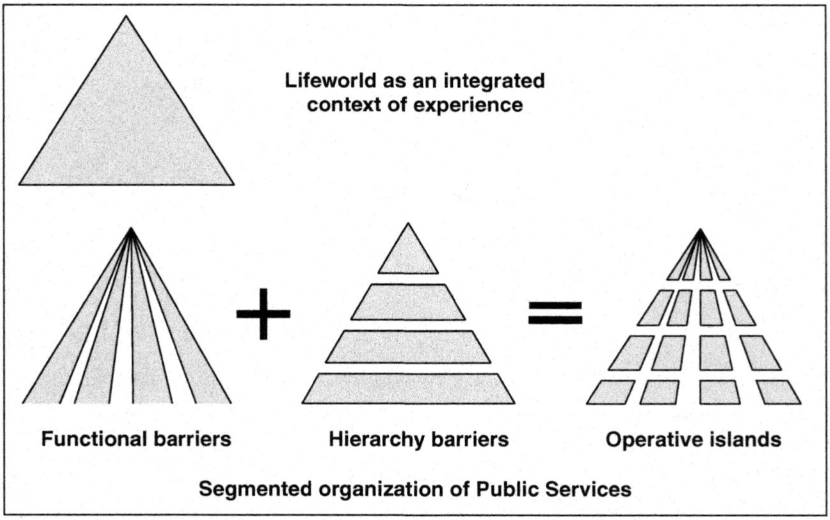

Source: modified in accordance with Hörrmann and Tiby 1991

Fig. 3.8 Pillarization and islandization of living environments and support institutions. (Source: Schubert, 2018a, 12)

welfare offices and the respective offices for schools, sports and culture, for construction matters, there is the building department and for vocational matters the 'Jobcenter', among others.

In order for participation to succeed, not the responsibility of the office should be considered central, but the person with disabilities instead. Pillarizations can be overcome and municipal participation landscapes can be developed if cooperation and networking take place on the following three levels (Schubert, 2018b) (Fig. 3.9).

1. Level: Political security through common meetings of municipal committees
    - In order to politically secure municipal participation landscapes, the municipal committees dealing with participation, such as social affairs, health, construction, education, culture, family, youth, etc., should cooperate with each other and coordinate along the principle of participation.
2. Level: Creation of structural networks between executives
    - Executives of the respective offices as well as voluntary organizations should network and make strategic decisions that help to enable participation.

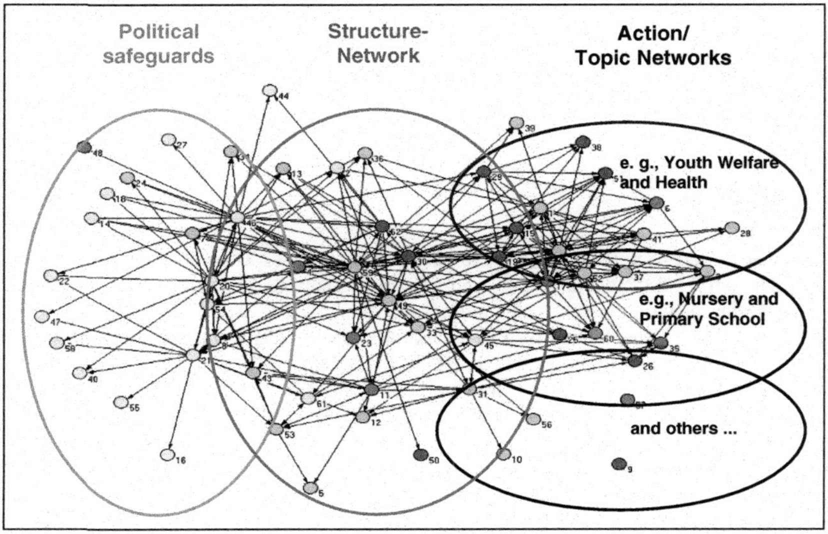

Own representation

Fig. 3.9 Cooperation and networking. (Source: Schubert, 2018b, 97)

3. Level: Creation of action networks between professionals
    - From the perspective of inclusion, action networks of professionals of public and private institutions should be created in order to make use of the resources in the social environment.
    - These professionals should become guides in the social welfare system and social space managers for people with disabilities.

3.3 Review Questions for Chap. 3

3.1 In what context did the term Corporate Governance originally arise?
3.2 What is the goal of the Corporate Governance Code?
3.3 What Principal-Agent-conflicts are there in the non-profit sector?
3.4 What do you understand by natural and artificial networks, respectively?
3.5 How can common action structures be established?
3.6 What are the limits in networking with organizations from other functional areas?
3.7 How can cooperation between different organizations take place?
3.8 Which interests are to be considered in governance processes between politics, businesses and associations?
3.9 Which factors are of particular importance for successful cooperation?
3.10 What is to be considered in decision-making processes?
3.11 What is meant by the "Degree of Connection"?

References

Aachener Erklärung des Deutschen Städtetages anlässlich des Kongresses „Bildung in der Stadt" am 22./23. November 2007, https://www.staedtetag.de/files/dst/docs/Dezernat-3/Archiv/aachener-erklaerung-2007.pdf. Zugegriffen: 5. Apr. 2021.

Auer, J. (2010). Hilfreich auch für kleine Organisationen – Der Kodex der Lebenshilfe hat sich bewährt. (S. 211 et seq.). *Blätter der Wohlfahrtspflege 6.*

Bachert, R. (2006). Was bedeutet Corporate Governance? In R. Bachert (Hrsg.), *Corporate Governance in Nonprofit-Unternehmen* (S. 14–26). WRS Verlag.

Baecker, D. (1994). Soziale Hilfe als Funktionssystem der Gesellschaft, Stn. 93–110. *Zeitschrift für Soziologie,* Heft 2.

Bangert, C. (2010). Geschäftsführung und Aufsicht trennen – Die Grundsätze verantwortungsvoller Unternehmensführung im Deutschen Caritasverband. (S. 207–210). *Blätter der Wohlfahrtspflege 6.*

Baums, T. (Hrsg.) (2001). Bericht der Regierungskommission Corporate Governance: Unternehmensführung, Unternehmenskontrolle, Modernisierung des Aktienrechts. O. Schmidt.

Beck, M. (2010). Organisationen gut und richtig führen. (S. 203–206). *Blätter der Wohlfahrtspflege 6.*

Becker, T., Dammer, I., Howaldt, J., & Loose, A. (2011). *Netzwerkmanagement*. Springer.

Bullinger, H., & Nowak, J. (1998). *Soziale Netzwerkarbeit. Eine Einführung für soziale Berufe*. Lambertus.

Bundesministerium für Familie, Senioren, Frauen und Jugend (Hrsg.) (2006). Zwölfter Kinder- und Jugendbericht, Bericht über die Lebenssituation junger Menschen und die Leistungen der Kinder- und Jugendhilfe in Deutschland, Berlin, Im Internet unter: https://www.bmfsfj.de/resource/blob/112224/7376e6055bbcaf822ec30fc6ff72b287/12-kinder-und-jugendbericht-data.pdf. Zugegriffen: 1. Sept. 2021

Corporate Governance Kodex Gute Unternehmensführung in der Lebenshilfe. Eine Empfehlung der Bundesvereinigung Lebenshilfe für Menschen mit geistiger Behinderung e. V. für ihre Mitgliedsorganisationen, Stand: Sommer 2012 Quelle: https://www.lebenshilfe.de/de/ueber-uns/aufgaben-und-ziele/Dateien/06-Corporate-Governance-Kodex-Lebenshilfe.php?listLink=1.

Deutscher Bundestag. (2005). Bericht über die Lebenssituation junger Menschen und die Leistungen der Kinder- und Jugendhilfe in Deutschland – Zwölfter Kinder- und Jugendbericht – Deutscher Bundestag Drucksache 15/6014 15. Wahlperiode 10.10.2005. http://dip21.bundestag.de/dip21/btd/15/060/1506014.pdf. Zugegriffen: 5. Apr. 2021.

difu (Deutsches Institut für Urbanistik) (Jekel, G. unter Mitarbeit von Beckmann, K.J., Arndt, P., Müller, K., Sander, R., Scheumann, D.) im Auftrag der Senatsverwaltung für Stadtentwicklung, Berlin (2007). Vorstudie zur Einrichtung einer „Netzwerkagentur Generationenübergreifendes Wohnen". *Sonderveröffentlichungen.* http://edoc.difu.de/edoc.php?id=COZ7M16W. Zugegriffen: 19. Aug. 2019.

Eberle, D. (2010). Governance in der politischen Ökonomie II: Corporate Governance. In Benz, A. & Dose, N. (Hrsg.), *Governance – Regieren in komplexen Regelsystemen* (2. Aufl., S. 155–173). VS Verlag.

Florian, F. (2008). Netzwerkarbeit. Die Netzwerkperspektive in der Praxis. In Schubert, H. (Hrsg.), *Netzwerkmanagement*. VS Verlag.

Handelsblatt vom 13.10.2015

Heinrich-Böll-Stiftung. (Hrsg.). (2011). Kommunale Bildungslandschaften. Ein Bericht von Anika Duveneck und Einblicke in die Praxis von Sybille Volkholz, Reihe Bildung und Kultur, Band 9. https://www.boell.de/sites/default/files/2012-02-Kommunale_Bildungslandschaften.pdf. Zugegriffen 05.04.2021.

Kolhoff, L., & Gebhardt, C. (Hrsg.) (2016). *Stadtteil in der Schule*. Springer VS.

Marschik, N. (2016). Anlagen zur Allgemeinen Erhebung in den Sozialräumen der Grundschule Altmühlstraße, Rheinring und Bebelhof. In L. Kolhoff & C. Gebhardt (Hrsg.), *Stadtteil in der Schule* (S. 234–239). Springer VS.

Mitchell, R. K., Agle, B. R., & Wood, D. J. (1997). Toward a Theory of Stakeholder Identification and Salience: Defining the Principle of Who and What Really Counts. *Academy of Management Review, 22. Jahrgang*, Heft 4, 853–896.

Riege, M., & Schubert, H. (Hrsg.). (2019). *Sozialraumanalyse. Grundlagen – Methoden – Praxis* (6. Aufl.). Verlag Sozial – Raum – Management.

Schubert H. (2018a). *Netzwerkorientierung in Kommune und Sozialwirtschaft. Eine Einführung.* Springer VS.

Schubert, H. (2018b). *Netzwerkmanagement in Kommune und Sozialwirtschaft. Eine Einführung.* Springer VS.

Schubert, H. (Hrsg.) (2008). *Netzwerkmanagement – Koordination von professionellen Vernetzungen – Grundlagen und Praxisbeispiele.* VS Verlag.

Schuhen, A. (2014). Corporate Governance in sozialwirtschaftlichen Organisationen. In U. Arnold, K. Grunwald, & B. Maelicke (Hrsg.), *Lehrbuch der Sozialwirtschaft* (S. 525–545). Nomos.

Siebart, P. (Hrsg.) (2006). *Corporate Governance von Nonprofit-Organisationen. Ausgewählte Aspekte der Organisation und Führung.* Haupt

Theuvsen, L. (2001). Stakeholder-Management – Möglichkeiten des Umgangs mit Anspruchsgruppen, Münsteraner Diskussionspapiere zum Nonprofit-Sektor 16. http://www.aktive-buergerschaft.de/fp_files/Diskussionspapiere/2001wp-band16. Zugegriffen: 10. Juni 2021.

Vester, F. (1993). *Unsere Welt – ein vernetztes System* (8. Aufl.). dtv.

Wald, A., & Jansen, D. (2007). Netzwerke. In Benz, A., Lütz, S., Schimank, U. & Simonis, G. (Hrsg.), *Handbuch governance* (S. 93–105). VS Verlag.

Weyer, J. (2000). *Soziale Netzwerke. Konzepte und Methoden der sozialwissenschaftlichen Netzwerkforschung.* Oldenbourg

Micro Level: "Interaction" 4

Abstract

On the micro level, the topic of governance is dealt with from the perspective of the actors and their interactions. Communication and trust, as well as the "chemistry" between actors, are important success factors for governance processes, as is the use of governance methods of participation, conflict resolution, balance of interests, and activation in social space.

Learning Objectives
In the following chapter, you will learn more about the interactions and interests of individual actors in governance processes. You will learn what social capital you bring with you as a "networker", how you act in social space and which principles of orientation in social space you should consider.

In addition, you will learn about governance methods suitable to encourage actors to engage in joint collective action.

4.1 Interactions in Governance Processes

Governance processes are characterized by the interaction of actors, bringing the interests and behavior of those involved into focus.

L. Kolhoff, *Governance in the Social Economy*,
https://doi.org/10.1007/978-3-658-38743-3_4

4.1.1 Considering The Actors' Interests

Governance is based on voluntary cooperation in which each actor pursues certain goals and is motivated by them. The involved actors' different logics of action have to be considered:

Logics of Action of the Involved Actors

- Municipal politicians are usually oriented towards territory because they have to take into account regional conditions if they want to be re-elected. They have to weigh which topics they want to include in their political agenda. They let themselves be guided by the code of the function system "politics" and, accordingly, follow the action logic of power.
- A company, on the other hand, wants to achieve the highest possible profit and therefore acts according to the action logics of market and price.
- Civil society coalitions, e.g., associations, follow logics of professional conduct or association politics, and due to their membership structure they are often territorially bound.

The interests of individual actors can differ considerably. Participants only act if their discernable benefit is greater than the costs. Governance processes lack the option to impose sanctions, and power can only be used very subtly, if at all. This is due to the fact that if conflicts arise and the effort or commitment is greater as a result, governance structures can quickly break down. Communication and trust as well as common goals and visions are decisive for successful cooperation.

Since the actors' interests often differ, governance can only work if the people involved know and trust each other. The "chemistry" between actors must therefore be right. This is a factor that is not easy to measure, but which becomes more tangible through answering the following questions:

Overview

Common goals and visions

- Which institutions have goals that at least partially coincide with our goals?

Willingness and ability to change perspective

- What interests and expectations does our partner have?
- What do we have to do to take our partner's perspective?

Embracing something new

- Who can we dispatch to do the governance work?
- Who is less blinkered and better able to embrace something new?

Mutual trust

- What do we need to do to maintain our trust so that others trust us, and what do we need to pay attention to so that we can trust others?

There can only be winners

- In which areas are there win-win situations?
- What do we need to do so that we are not exploited, and at which points do we need to be careful not to exploit others?

Common communication

- How can others understand us?
- Are our terms and expectations clear to others?
- What do we need to do to make our expectations clear to others?

Regular contact care

- Have we maintained contact to our partners?
- What do we have to do to maintain contact? (Endes, 2001, 103 et seq.)

Governance is a process of decision-making. We need to analyze which actors take on which roles in decision processes (Speckbacher & Pfaffenzeller, 2004, p. 196). It's important to keep in mind that decisions are rarely determined by formal procedures because when it comes to voting in decision-making bodies, the crucial factors have often already been decided. It should also be noted that many decision-makers seek advice beforehand. Advisers are not elected delegates but people who are attributed competence. They are able to influence processes and should therefore be involved early on.

Preliminary decisions

It must be asked where, when, in which bodies, and – most importantly – under whose influence preliminary decisions are made.

In which informal places and at which informal times are decisions prepared, and how are these decisions influenced, whether by individuals or, for example, by the targeted use or omission of information?

Many governance processes demand that participants not only engage selectively, but in a sustained manner. Therefore, initiators of governance processes should maintain social relations and contacts once they have been established. It is especially important to foster relationships with key stakeholders (Speckbacher & Pfaffenzeller, 2004, p. 203).

4.1.2 Developing Social Capital

The social capital of the individuals involved is essential for governance processes. An indicator of an actor's social capital is his "degree of connection", that is, the number and quality of his relationships within the network.

Successful governance actors are successful networkers and should develop their social capital as such, following these recommendations:

What you should do

- A networker's contacts are his capital.
  - You should establish and maintain contacts.
- Organizations participate in networks when they expect to receive added value.
  - An organization may not be aware of what it gets or could get from the network. You should make this clear.

- Since no one can be forced to participate in a network, you should always communicate on equal footing and express appreciation.
  - You should never denigrate anyone.
- Networks often develop as part of roundtable discussions.
  - You should utilize existing events and structures or encourage the creation of new forums for communication.

Relationships do not emerge on their own. Therefore, the initiators of governance processes should, in addition to team skills, communication skills and social competence, have the ability to generate sympathy and repeatedly identify and develop new options in accordance with the categorical imperative of the networker: "Act at all times in such a way that others can join in the results of your actions" (Sloterdijk, 2004, p. 488). There are different approaches and types, which Heuberger (Heuberger, 2007, p. 77 et seq.) distinguishes as follows:

1. The grassroots networker: I have experienced and introduced to each other so many people that it would suffice for 1.000 lifetimes.
2. The truffle pig: I have developed a general sense for patterns and trends.
3. The project mediator who acts according to the motto: "I connect the right people and ideas with each other."

4.1.3 Acting in Social Space

Governance processes are often located in social space. In social space, it is necessary to initiate and maintain relationships within social networks.

Support and Initiate Social Networks

An important task in the context of social work is to stabilize existing networks and to activate new spatial networks. It should be noted that relationships do not simply emerge because people live next to each other. Although people can and want to do something together if they like each other, in some cases an active neighborhood develops, but not in others (Häußermann & Siebel, 2004, p. 115). Spatial relationships emerge through interactions that are based on social homogeneity, social status, life goals, etc. The probability of close neighborhood relationships is higher within socially homogeneous neighborhoods than within heterogeneous neighborhoods, while unwanted contacts promote distance (Häußermann & Siebel, 2004, p. 111 et seq.).

This phenomenon is exacerbated by changes in community structures. While in the 19th and 20th centuries, community was defined by spatial reference—communication took place from door to door, one talked to neighbors and built spatial community structures (door-to-door community)—today, communities can be detached from any spatial reference through communication and transport media. Contact with neighbors loses importance. At the same time, the household itself becomes more important (Straus, 2004, p. 8). One can make phone calls at home, watch TV, eat, drink, sleep, and one doesn't necessarily have to spend one's free time with the neighbors, but can spend it with the people one chooses. These changes also have an impact on public places. They lose their character as places that promote community and instead become traffic junctions or shopping areas. But the process continues. While telephones and cars still connected places (place-to-place community), modern communication tools such as cell phones, the internet and social networks completely dissolve spatial reference because people can be in different places–in a car, on a train–and still communicate with each other (person-to-person community). This trend leads to the fact that it is no longer the space but the virtual network which increasingly becomes the focus of social contacts (Straus, 2004). Consequently, dispersed neighborhoods should be sponsored. For when it comes to neighborhood contacts, what is important is not so much the spatial structure, but the quality and voluntariness of personal relationships (Seifert, 2012, p. 168). Therefore, one of the essential keypoints of social work oriented towards the social environment is to develop and stabilize personal networks, taking into account the following principles of socio-spatial orientation developed by Hinte (Hinte & Treeß, 2007, 2008) (Fig. 4.1).

Observing the Basic Principles of Socio-spatial Orientation

1. **Orientation towards the will of the people**
   The starting point of any socio-spatial work is the will of the people, distinguished from naive desires. While in the case of desires it is expected that something will be done or produced, the will is an attitude from which an activity is pursued (Hinte & Treeß, 2007, p. 46); that is, whenever someone expresses their will, they are willing to do something and also willing to use their own resources. What is important is to inquire into their personal interestes and needs instead of just inferring them. Individuals have their own solutions which must be developed and made to fit the respective living conditions. Activating the will means counteracting learned helplessness (Seligmann, 1995). It should not be talked about what people desire, but what they want

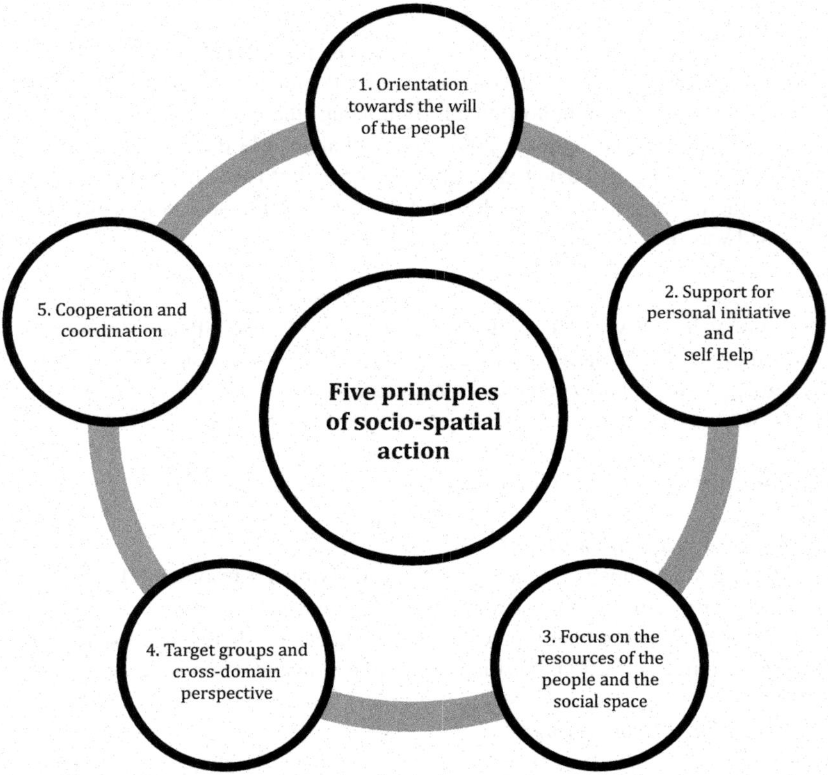

Fig. 4.1 Five principles of social-spatial action (own representation)

and to what they are also willing to commit their efforts. Listening to people attentively to find out what they want is especially important. What motivates them? What are they devoting themselves to, what do they want to change, and which cause are they willing to contribute to? Based on the will, it is then necessary to develop joint plans with the people, in which they, but also others, contribute to success.

2. **Support of self-initiative and self-help**
   The second principle is support of self-initiative and self-help (Hinte & Treeß, 2007, 51 et seq.). This principle gives priority to activating work before care work. Furthermore, the principle requires that those affected by these decisions are to be involved in the decision-making process.

3. **Focus on resources**
   A third principle is "focus on the resources of people and the social environment" (Hinte and Treeß 2007, 60 et seq.) People are considered resource-oriented and not deficit-oriented. Following the empowerment approach (Herriger, 2014; Theunissen, 2009; Kulig et al., 2011) the focus is on identifying, activating and using skills and resources with which people can shape both their own paths through life and their own living spaces in a self-determined way, i.e., gain control over their own lives.

> The question is: What strengths do people have? What skills and resources do they or their relatives, friends, acquaintances, neighbors and network partners have and how can they be activated?

Empowerment takes place on different levels:

Subject-oriented Empowerment
Subject-oriented empowerment supports an individual's resources. It comprises personal approaches to improving self-esteem and self-efficacy. Methods used include strength-based biographical work, competence dialogue, resource diagnostics, resource activation, personal future planning and competence training.

Group-oriented Empowerment
Group-oriented empowerment is dedicated to connecting people who have similar problems, concerns or interests in order to overcome processes of isolation and enable joint action. Methods such as network diagnosis, networking, promotion of self-help groups, promotion of peer support and peer counseling are used.

Organization-related Empowerment
Organization-related empowerment takes place mainly in the context of participation processes, e.g., within self-help groups or interest groups.

Social space-related empowerment promotes resources on site, i.e., resources in local districts. This includes neighborhoods in particular.

4. **Comprehensive target group perspective and cross-departmental perspective**
   The fourth principle requires a cross-departmental perspective based on comprehensive target groups (Hinte & Treeß, 2007, 72 et seq.). It is about thinking and acting comprehensively. Synergies should be promoted and competen-

cies and resources from other areas than the social sector, such as culture and leisure or even urban development, should be used while networks should be built including people, groups and organizations with similar needs.

5. **Cooperation and coordination**
   The fifth principle is "cooperation and coordination" (Hinte & Treeß 2007, 75 et seq.). It is about winning over and activating as many professional and voluntary actors as possible, communicating and cooperating with each other, and building networks.

Now that interactions in governance processes have been addressed, the following section deals with governance methods.

4.2 Governance Methods

Governance methods include methods of research, participation, ideation, conflict resolution, and activation.

Action research is one of the research methods used in governance processes.

4.2.1 Action Research

Action research, founded by Kurt Lewin, is a type of professional research that is deliberately and directly focused on solving practical social problems. "The research required for social praxis can best be characterized as research in the service of social enterprises and social technology. It is a type of science of action […], a comparative study of the conditions and effects of different forms of social action. It is itself a type of research that leads to social action. Research which produces nothing but books is not enough" (Lewin, 1953, p. 280). The action research model requires the cooperation of scientists and practitioners in the design and evaluation of research. Researchers and those seeking advice and assistance form a joint action system. The affected are not research objects, but the researchers' cooperating and interacting partners.

Various methods are used in action research projects. The survey feedback method, which goes back to Lewin, has proven to be particularly effective. When using this method, data is collected and relationships are researched (survey), e.g., using questionnaires, interviews, case studies, group discussions, etc. The results of this data collection are reflected back to the affected themselves (feedback) and are discussed and diagnosed. Afterwards, changes are proposed and action plans are developed and implemented.

The survey feedback method is therefore characterized by three steps (Fig. 4.2):

In the context of governance, action research can be used to set in motion change processes within a social space and in cooperation with the people affected. Tools of action research include activating surveys as an entry point to capture competencies in the social environment, or the observation of social spaces, by which observable facts (such as streetscape, traffic, but also interactions in social space) are recorded. These methods serve to form hypotheses and as preparation for a social space analysis through which objective facts, opinion and attitudes about the social environment can be determined. Where do people feel affected? Where are possibilities or potentials for change that could be used? Are there informal leaders in the social space?

In a preliminary study, the devised hypothesis is then checked for the first time. For this purpose, experts and participants are interviewed. The survey's written results are then processed and analyzed in order to prepare the main study.

The main study consists of the levels "expert survey" and "affected survey".

The main study's results are presented to the participants with the aim of activating them to participate in problem-solving processes (Fig. 4.3).

To participate and activate, very diverse methods can be used, as shown below.

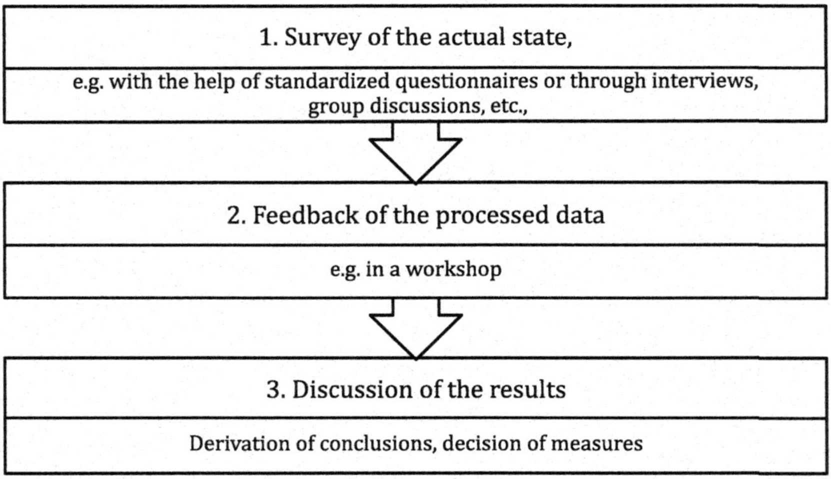

Fig. 4.2 Survey feedback method (author's representation)

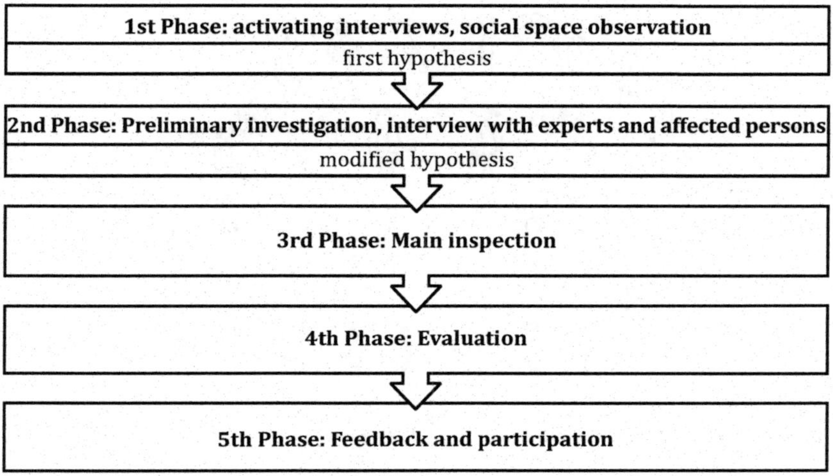

Fig. 4.3 The action research process (author's representation)

4.2.2 Participation Methods

Conducting Discussion Events

The most commonly used participation method consists of discussion events in the form of a "Hearing Discussion" with experts. This form is appropriate to present expert opinions on certain subject matters. In order to involve the participants, however, other forms are more suitable, such as the frequently used "Metaplan Moderation Method", in which discussion results are visualized using cards (Kühl, 2009, 195 et seq.), or the less frequently used "Fishbowl Technique" (Fig. 4.4).

"In a fishbowl, an inner and an outer circle of chairs are set up. If a participant from the outer circle (audience) wants to participate in the discussion, they must either sit on a free chair in the inner circle (discussant) or stand behind an occupied chair. The person sitting on that chair may conclude their remarks but has to leave the inner circle afterwards. The other person then takes this place." (Source: World Cafe, Fishbowl and Open Space, Alternatives to Traditional Conference Models, https://blog.converia.de/de/world-cafe-fish-bowl-und-open-space/)

Like the fishbowl technique, the "network carousel" also uses an inner and an outer circle.

Fig. 4.4 Fishbowl. (Source: https://ceimzeit.de/fishbowl-methode/)

"In this arrangement, one half of the participants takes a seat in the inner circle (facing outwards) and the other half takes one in the outer circle (facing inwards)—the people sit opposite each other in pairs. In the first carousel conversation, the person in the inner circle exchanges views on a given question with the person sitting opposite in the outer circle. The most important answers are noted on—at least two—metaplan cards. After a while (time limit depends on the depth of the question), the inner circle rotates clockwise to form the next pair conversation and before the following carousel conversation, the outer circle rotates counterclockwise. As a result of the position changes, the participants come into conversation with different partners over several rounds. During each new round, the moderators attach all Metaplan cards with notes of the previous conversation round to the pinboards.

A specific question can be formulated for each round; however, the question can remain the same for all rounds. […]

After a certain number of rounds, the two circles are dissolved. Now the participants of the inner circle and the outer circle, who have not yet talked to each other, form three-person groups (triads). Together they look at the results on the pinboards and come to an agreement about the most important aspects, using a synthesis-oriented question—for example: 'What three conclusions do you draw from your conversations and the pinned cards?' Finally, the teams present their findings and pin them to an empty pinboard." (Schubert, 2021, 12 et seq.)

Activations can also be achieved in classical plenary sessions by means of appropriate methods, such as:

- "Buzz groups" (2–3 participants exchange views on a given question for about 5 min.)
- "Corner discussion" (In the corners of the room, prepared posters are hung up on which half-sentences are to be completed.)
- "Interviews in small groups" (In order to better get to know each other, participants interview each other in small groups (2–4 people) and introduce the interviewed partners to the plenum.)
- "Vernissage" (The participants are asked to create a picture or even a sculpture on a topic.) (cf. Higher Education Didactics, Methodenbar https://www.uni-due.de/imperia/md/content/zfh/methodenbar_2012.pdf). Accessed: 1.09.2021

Methods for the Participation of Large Groups

In addition to structured discussion events, open procedures for large groups (such as Open Space, World Café or future conferences) can be used to involve, firstly, citizens who are not members of representative bodies in citizen forums or district conferences, and secondly, external and internal stakeholders of social economy organizations.

Open Space

"Open Space [English] means 'open space' or 'free space'. It is a method that is used to design conferences. The method allows for work with small to large groups (8 to 1,000 people or more). It is also used as a tool for organizational development. Open Space is based on the principles of self-organization and self-determination of the participating individuals as well as on a fundamental departure from control. Thus, the use of the Open Space method should maximize influence and participation of the actual participants of a conference. In contrast to traditional conferences, there is no pre-planned conference program in Open Space, that is, no fixed schedule. A schedule is outlined by the participants at the beginning of the event itself. Only a (leading) topic is given. Open Space serves as a methodology for problem solving, it offers a rough structure for the implementation of problem solving processes. However, no strategy for solving an existing problem in an organization is predetermined. No person should know or want to determine the results of such a conference in advance. There are many different topics and areas of application of the method. Open Space is used especially when dealing with complex and urgent problems, for example, the quick and creative

design of change processes in organizations. The method can be implemented in many different types of organizations (profit and non-profit sector). The duration of an Open Space conference can range from a few hours (e.g., regular departmental meetings) to several days (e.g., conference for initiating changes in an organization)". (Reich 2008)

World-Café

"The World Café—developed by American *management consultants Juanita Brown and David Isaacs—is a globally used dialogue and workshop method. It is suitable for group sizes of 12 to 2,000 participants.*

Based on the assumption that there is collective knowledge, people should be brought into a constructive conversation with each other on topics that are relevant to the participants. The aim is to allow as many stakeholders as possible to have their say and thus to enable them to contribute and participate. The World Café approach promotes self-development and self-control as well as self-organization. Conversations take place in a relaxed coffeehouse atmosphere and aim to make common knowledge and collective intelligence visible in order to develop new perspectives, ways of thinking and options for action.

The standard procedure for a World Café takes approximately two to three hours: Participants are seated in the room at tables with four to five people. The tables are covered with white, writable tablecloths and pens or markers. A facilitator *or* moderator, *acting as host, introduces the working method at the beginning, explains the procedure and points out the rules of conduct–the café etiquette. During the event two or three different questions are processed at all tables in consecutive conversation rounds of 15–30 min. Between the conversation rounds, the groups mix anew. Only the hosts remain at their tables the entire time: They welcome new guests, summarize the previous conversation briefly and get the discussion going again. The World Café closes with a reflection phase."* (Söllner n.d., 2010)

Future Conference (Fig. 4.5)

"In a future conference (Future Search), 60–80 people of different interest groups come together to address a common issue that no one of them can solve on their own. Together they develop a common, consensus-based vision of the future and plan concrete steps for its implementation."

A future conference begins with the participants getting to know each other, followed by a review of the past. This review creates a sense of community and forms an important basis for all subsequent phases. Then, for the first time, participants look to the future and compile what will come at them from the outside, what they need to prepare for and what they need to be prepared. This establishes relation-

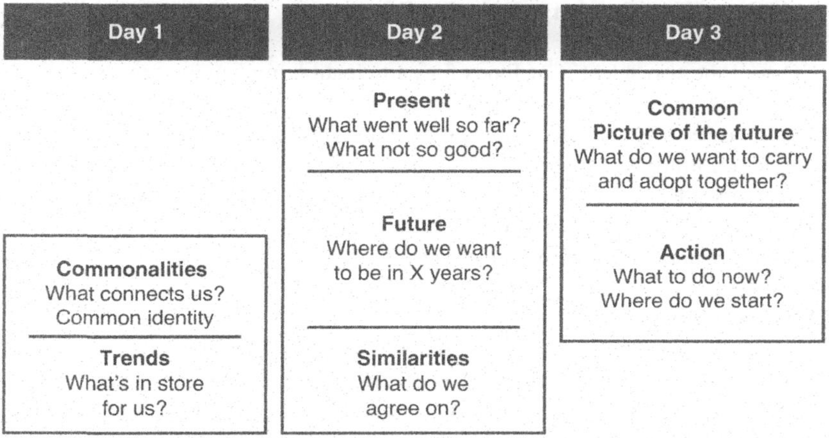

Fig. 4.5 Outline of a future conference

ships and makes it clear to everyone where future challenges lie. Energy for joint action is generated.

"On the morning of the second day, the current situation is examined. What is already going well, what is looking less good? What can they be proud of and what do they perhaps regret? What do they want to take with them into a shared future, what rather leave behind? Then, it is time to design a shared vision of the future. First, small groups envision and create a vivid and lively image of the state they would like to achieve in X years. In creative staging, these visions of the future become alive and conceivable for everyone. On the second evening and the following morning, the most important step towards a shared future is taken: the similarities in the different visions of the future are brought to light and turned into a vision shared by all. In the final phase, based on this foundation, measures, activities and projects are planned." (*Agonda* 2009–2016)

In addition to this event for large groups, there is a wealth of other participation methods from which methods for participation in planning processes are selected. They cover a broad spectrum between participatory and representative approaches.

Methods for Participation in Planning Processes

Planning cell

One of the two selected methods for participation in planning processes is the planning cell (Dienel, 2005). It consists of citizens who participate in planning as representatives of an affected population group. These citizens are not elected, but selected according to various objective criteria. The procedure is illustrated using the example of a citizen's opinion of the city of Aachen. This citizen's opinion was prepared by 94 citizens who participated for a total of eight days (12–15 and 19–22 November 2007) in four planning cells.

The Procedure

The planning cell procedure is a tool to facilitate participation of citizens in political decision-making processes. It was developed at the Bergische Universität of Wuppertal in the early 1970s and has since been used extensively at national and international levels. The guiding principle of the planning cell is to give citizens the opportunity to constructively contribute their opinion, their life experience and their expertise to political decision-making processes. The development of a new waste disposal ordinance in consultation with the citizens through the planning cell expressly does not mean planning "from above or top-down". Rather, specific measures are developed together with those affected, who, from their point of view, can contribute to improving the local living conditions. The results of planning cells give an indication of which change strategies citizens expect and in which measures they are willing to actively participate.

Random Selection of Participants

A planning cell consists of approximately 25 people who are selected at random from the population register of a municipality. Random selection increases the acceptability of results because the participants come from all parts of society. Some people who have never before participated in political activities are involved this way. A "colorful" mixture ensures that people who normally have no contact talk with each other.

Multi-day, Intense and Task-oriented Work

The citizen experts work for four days on the task at hand according to a fixed work schedule. The work schedule allows for the necessary time for information, discussion and decision-making, but at the same time, it is also a limiting framework that prevents the discussion from spiraling out of control. For their work, the citizen experts are remunerated and released from their routine obligations. Since the activity is time-limited, the participants do not develop any self-interest beyond their expert assessment.

Neutral Organization and Supervision of the Procedure
The procedure is necessarily open-ended. Preparation, implementation and evaluation are in the hands of the implementing body.

Structured Work Schedule
The methodological process of the planning cell is precisely structured. The implementing body divides the task at hand into individual, thematically specified work units. Each work unit is divided into time steps with exactly measured time intervals. All planning cells work according to the same schedule.

Information by Experts
The citizen experts are informed by experts from science, associations and interest groups about the various topics. Where appropriate, several speakers are used so that controversial viewpoints are provided. The lectures serve as an impulse for the discussion of the citizens, whose everyday knowledge is supplemented by the experts' factual information.

Politician Hearing
The politician hearing offers the opportunity for a fact-oriented, moderated discussion between citizens and representatives of all parties.

Discussion in Small Groups
The individual problems and pieces of information are discussed exclusively in a small, unmoderated group. Discussions in small groups promote the formation of opinion on the part of the citizen experts and put the factual information received in relation to their personal experiences. Even people who are not very experienced in conversation express their opinions in small groups. The small groups are newly assembled before each work unit according to a rotation principle. This prevents the formation of opinion leadership and facilitates fair discussion. The results of the work in small groups are presented and collected in the plenum. Afterwards, each participant has the opportunity to evaluate all recommendations individually by awarding points.

Neutrality in Moderation
The moderators lead through the work schedule, explain the procedures of individual work units and pay attention to the timetable. They do not influence the content of the program or the communication of any factual information.

The Opinion

Results and evaluations produced by the citizen experts are summarized in the form of a citizen opinion. This opinion contains a description of the task and the procedure, as well as a presentation of the selection process and the course of the planning cells. At the opinion's core is the condensed and analyzed data in the form of texts, numbers and tables. In this way, the entire process of creating the citizen opinion is made transparent and comprehensible. Before publication, the citizen opinion is checked by representatives of the planning cells.

(Citizen opinion Aachen, Aachen, 2008, p. 14–16, source: http://www.oegut.at/downloads/pdf/p_buergergutachten-aachen.pdf) Accessed: 1.09.2021

Lawyer Participation

Another method is lawyer participation, in which marginalized groups frequently are at the center. These groups are provided with a competent person (lawyer function) who helps them formulate their ideas and goals, and who represents the interests of these groups. The lawyer function can only be carried out if it is kept free from dependencies and role conflicts. Lawyer planning was used, e.g., by the city of Hanover in urban development:

Lawyer Participation in Urban Development

In 1995, the city of Hanover had decided in a council solution to involve its citizens in the city's further development. This was to be achieved by handing over questions of urban development to an attorney planning scheme. The Citizen's Office for Urban Development was established in order to lend support.

Location: Hanover

Started: September 1995

Background

Through the Citizen's Office for Urban Development, the city wants to contribute to the public discussion of problems and projects. Its work is financed mostly by the city, but the office is nevertheless independent in substance and organization.

Goal

The goal is to improve the involvement of citizens in planning and processes, inter alia by strengthening their active involvement in local projects.

The Citizen's Office for Urban Development contributes to an open, transparent and flexible planning process, and it supervises this process by means of a staff trained in methodology.

Process

The office's employees take up suggestions, questions and problems from citizens and forward them to the authorities responsible or they carry out their own research. Initiatives, groups and associations have the opportunity to exchange information or coordinate activities via the office. If desired, they are supported in doing so. In addition, the Citizen's Office for Urban Development also deals with questions of urban development on its own initiative and supports other activities and processes, for example, within the framework of the local Agenda 21. In addition, comprehensive participation projects for young people are developed at the district level. There are also specialist forums, for example on the topic of the "child-friendly city". Furthermore, the office deals with the topic of housing quality through publications, lecture series and excursions and tries to give impulses towards the formation of broad coalitions.

Results

Despite problems with financing, the district office continues to work on the above-mentioned topics and has already been able to support numerous projects in their implementation.

External Links

http://www.bbs-hannover.de/

Contact

Citizen's office for urban development
Braunstr. 28
D-30169 Hannover
Telephone: (05 11) 7 00 09 34
Telefax: (05 11) 7 01 07 60
E-Mail: buergerbuero-stadtentwicklung(at)t-online.de

(Attorney planning in urban development in Hanover, last edited: 12.06.2013, author: Ulrich Rüttgers http://www.beteiligungskompass.org/article/show/804)

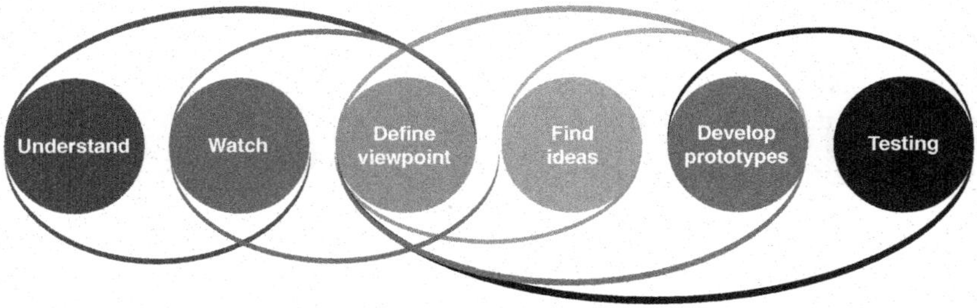

Fig. 4.6 The design thinking process. (Source: https://hpi-academy.de/design-thinking/was-ist-design-thinking.html Accessed: 1.9.2021)

4.2.3 Methods of Idea Generation and Solution Methods

Design Thinking

A currently much discussed method of finding solutions to complex challenges is design thinking. It is one of several approaches to deal with the intertwined challenges of the modern "VUCA" world[1] and is used primarily in the digital economy. Interdisciplinary teams try to find solutions to problems using creative methods. The focus is on user needs and requirements.

The method is based on the work of designers, which is understood to be a combination of understanding, observation, ideation, refinement, execution and learning (Fig. 4.6).

Design Thinking: Understanding, Observing, Defining Perspectives, Generating Ideas, Developing and Testing Prototypes

- "Understand: During the phase of understanding, teams delineate the problem area.
- Observe: During the phase of observation, participants look outward and build empathy for users and people affected.

[1] The term "VUCA" refers to volatile, insecure, complex and ambiguous environments (Hofert, 2016, p. 235). The term originally comes from the military, which must deal with a completely changed threat situation in times of cyber attacks and asymmetric warfare.

- Defining perspective: During this phase, everything is about defining the perspective. Gained insights are brought together and condensed.
- Generating ideas: During this phase, teams first develop a variety of solutions and then focus in on one.
- Developing prototypes: Subsequent prototyping advances the development of concrete solutions that can be tested on the appropriate target groups." (HPI Academy o. J.)

Design thinkers work with glue guns, cards, moderation walls and all kinds of other things to create creative solutions.

Classic creativity techniques, however, should not be left unmentioned.

Creativity Techniques

Brainstorming

All spontaneous thoughts that come to the participants' minds on a given topic or problem area are collected without evaluative comments. Even the most outlandish ideas should be articulated so that as many diverse and original solutions to a problem as possible can be found.

The group should not be too large; a group size of 6–8 people is ideal. Before the actual brainstorming begins, the group determines what the exact process will be and how much time it will approximately take. The goal is to develop as many ideas as possible, all individual contributions should be kept short. The group elects a moderator who observes compliance with the brainstorming rules:

The moderator keeps the flow of ideas going, ensures compliance with the rules and stops the session when the flow of ideas has dried up. The brainstorming should not take too long, but certainly as long as there is a flow of ideas. After this point, there is a short break.

In a follow-up step, all ideas can be sorted and evaluated according to their usefulness by the same or by another team.

Brainwriting

In brainwriting, each member of the idea-generating group writes down their ideas or alternative solutions on a sheet of paper (or a specially prepared form) and passes it on.

Worksheet

Task ____________________ ____________________		Sheet No: Date:

A variation of brainwriting is also known as ***Method 635***.

- Here, each member of a six-person group writes three ideas on a form, which is then passed on five times. Each participant writes down three ideas. The sheets are passed on clockwise. Now each participant can get inspiration from the ideas of their predecessors, supplement an already existing idea and develop it further, or they come up with new ideas. The working sheets are passed on until each participant has noted ideas on each working sheet.
- Then, as in brainstorming, all ideas are discussed and systematically evaluated by the same or by another group.

Mind map

A mind map is a form of representation that can give texts and thoughts a clear structure. A term that describes a problem or topic is placed at the center. With each mind map, note-taking begins with the central idea in the middle of the page. Around this center, a kind of map of thoughts, feelings, memories or plans and desires develops. Starting from the central idea, sections are associated which are related to this idea. The most important aspects are written on lines that are connected to the central idea (so-called main branches). The main branches are subdivided into sub-branches (so-called side branches or branches).

Frequently, governance is not only about participation and problem-solving but also about dealing with different interests which can lead to conflicts. Mediation is an effective tool for conflict resolution and interest balancing method. It can be brought to bear between institutions and individuals as well as between institutions and within them.

4.2.4 Mediation as a Method of Conflict Resolution and Balancing of Interests

In the United States, mediation has long been established as a complementary method of conflict resolution and reconciliation of interests, while in Germany it has only been discussed since the early 1990s. In the Federal Republic of Germany, conflicts are usually decided by courts according to the law and in a resource-intensive way, with lawyers trying to sway the judgement. The lawyers' toolbox consists of techniques meant to represent reality in such a way that it appears favorable for their own party and unfavorable for the opposing party. Legal disputes are, therefore, about victory and defeat, and their conflict resolution mechanism is collusive. Any legal decision is a delegated decision because it is made by a third party. In contrast, the parties involved in mediation try to develop common, viable solutions while taking into account existing legal norms.

Mediative conflict resolution and reconciliation of interests can be used between two people, within groups (e.g., in organizations) or between institutions (e.g., in the form of mediative arbitration).

Mediation is intended to promote capacities for dialogue, cooperation and design so as to develop fair, satisfactory, viable and legally binding agreements by utilizing the support of a mediator. In contrast to legal proceedings, mediation is not about victory or defeat, attack or defense, but about joint negotiation and thus about cooperation and consensus.

Mediators are intermediaries in a conflict and as such are not responsible for the conflict's resolution or the reconciliation of interests. Instead, they are responsible for the procedure itself. The solutions are worked out by the partners themselves. A mediators' tasks are to create a decision-making space, a constructive conversation atmosphere and to structure action processes in order to constructively resolve conflicts.

All parties to the conflict enter into mediation voluntarily and are responsible for its outcome. They should not be pressured by either side to achieve results, not be restricted in their self-determination, be able to perceive their own interests and needs, stand up for themselves and not be represented by lawyers. Decisions are not delegated to judges.

All parties to the conflict must be sufficiently informed, i.e., have the opportunity to recognise and weigh up all the information that is relevant to a decision, in order to be fully aware of its consequences. At the same time, all those involved are obliged not to make use of information gained in mediation in any legal proceedings.

All parties to the conflict must have a real interest in resolving the conflict and be able to express their interests and needs. There must be no extreme power differences between the partners.

Mediators are expected to maintain an impartial, neutral attitude towards the parties. This entails that they do not appear as witnesses in a court case or represent the parties as lawyers. They serve a process management function and are responsible for the design of the mediation process as well as the creation of suitable conditions. They also have a catalytic function, accelerating processes and forming a bridge of understanding between the parties to the conflict. In addition to mastering management techniques, they need mental strength because the parties to the conflict often harbor aggression and resentful feelings towards each other and it takes time for them to focus on themselves and articulate their own interests.

Since the qualifications of mediators are not clearly regulated and, consequently, lawyers, psychologists, social pedagogues, etc., pour into this field, uniform results cannot be expected from mediation.

The concept of mediation should be understood in a context oriented towards systemic learning. It promotes learning processes in the sense of self-responsible, joint change, and thus co-evolutionary action. As a co-evolutionary approach, mediation is based on finding solutions that are fruitful for both parties in the sense of a "win-win" strategy. It is about empowering people to see conflicts as an opportunity for acts of learning. A key method of mediation is therefore to perceive conflicts not negatively, but as functional for the system, in order to develop new ways that are also functional, but constructive.

From identifying problems through planning and strategic design of a mediation session to its execution with the mediators in mind, processes are treated in a similar context as in systemic family therapy or systemic and learning-oriented organizational development. Therefore, methods of systemic family therapy such as circular questioning, reframing, positive connotation, paradoxical intervention, etc., are used in mediation, too. In contrast to therapy, however, mediation is not about healing or processing psychological conflicts but about negotiating well-defined facts.

The mediators' task is to catalyze processes and initiate a new stable state at the current instability point of a system. They are oriented towards the participants without being partial (Table 4.1).

The mediation process is based on a phase model consisting of preparation, diagnosis, conflict resolution, implementation and evaluation phases (Fig. 4.7).

Before mediation begins, all parties to the conflict must choose a mediator. Mediators explain their own role and tasks, as well as the method's rules and

Table 4.1 Mediation methods (author's representation)

Conflict partner	Mediator
• Letting others express themselves without interruption • No insults or violence • I-messages • "Win-win" strategy • Perceive conflicts as functional phenomena • Perceive conflicts as an opportunity for acts of learning	• Active listening • Only intervene if necessary • Individual conversations • Idea generation techniques • Circular questions • Positive connotation • Paradoxical intervention • Connectivity/compatibility • Disturb the client's stuck system • Catalytically accelerate processes • Introduce and record a new stable state

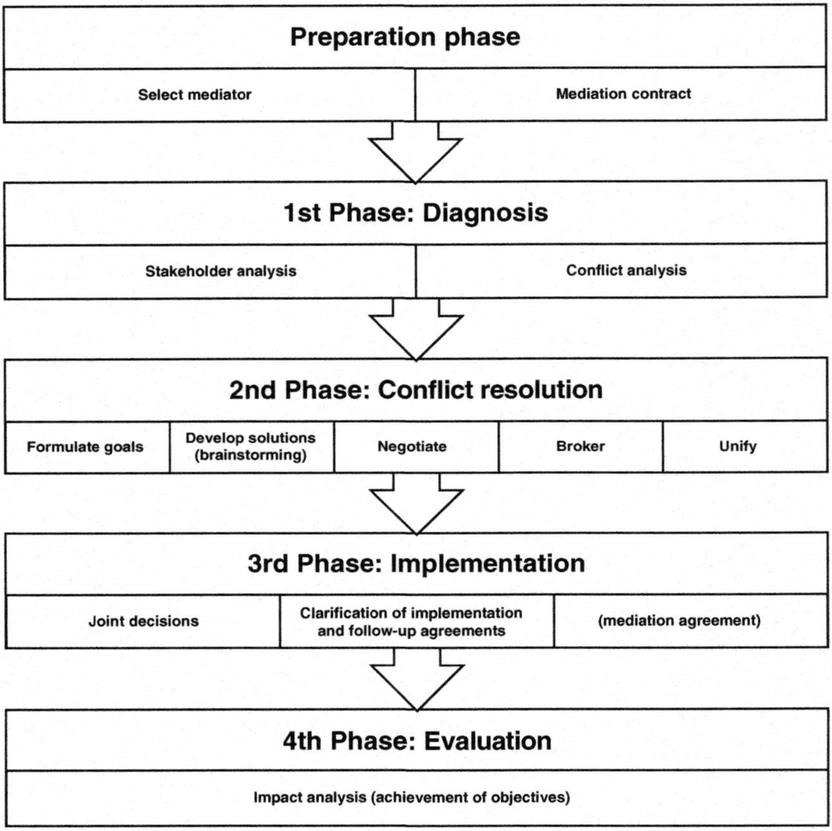

Fig. 4.7 Steps of mediation (author's representation)

goals, and they point out the advantages and disadvantages, alternatives as well as opportunities and risks. They explain the process, the costs and the requirements of mediation and ascertain motivation and suitability of all parties to the conflict. Once the parties are ready for mediation, the points of the conflict resolution are determined and a mediation agreement is made.

The diagnosis phase serves to collect information and to identify the issues in dispute. The diagnosis phase includes, in a first step, the stakeholder analysis. Here, the question arises as to who is involved in the conflict and to what extent the conflict is functional for stabilizing the relationship. Through their neutrality and through techniques such as paradoxical intervention, mediators gain access to the system. They try to find out the functionality of the conflict in order to disturb the collusive system.

Diagnosis features conflict analysis in particular. The parties concerned explain their view of the conflict. This also includes hidden feelings and backgrounds as well as subjective needs, interests and desires. Through active listening mediators make sure that the description of the conflict is complete. In order to be able to describe and analyze the conflict in detail, they use the technique of circular questions. Its aim is to define and describe differences in order to obtain a nuanced picture of the conflict situation.

As part of the conflict analysis, there is direct communication between the parties to the conflict, which is a prerequisite for the development of a conflict solution.

During the conflict resolution phase, in a first step, the mediation's goals (taking into account the factual, relational and process level) and, in a second step, solutions in the sense of appropriate courses of action are developed. For this purpose, ideation techniques (brainstorming, mind mapping, etc.) are used. Kuhn demands that solutions be described in detail. For this purpose, mediators should focus on interests and resources (Kuhn, 1999, p. 56). Several hypothetical solutions are drafted, and based on these hypotheses, solution paths are played through and evaluated.

The implementation phase is about implementing agreed-upon solutions. In addition to content-related and financial aspects, the law must also be taken into account. An implementation plan is drawn up, complete with nuanced agreements, responsibilities and implementation steps. There should be transactional balance. The result is documented as a mediation agreement in the form of a contract which is then signed.

The evaluation phase serves to check and correct the agreement. Based on verifiable indicators for target achievement, an impact analysis is carried out in order to examine whether the mediation's goals have been achieved.

The mediation approach can be used in governance relations, e.g., in the case of location decisions for large-scale projects, in environmental protection or in urban renewal, whenever individuals or citizen initiatives are involved (for example, in the case of institutionalized citizen participation by way of district committees, citizen conferences or public hearings. Techniques such as planning cells, future conferences or district conferences are the methods associated with this approach, as are arbitration proceedings. A well-known example was the "arbitration Stuttgart 21".

Stuttgart 21

*"It is the most controversial construction project in Germany: the conversion of Stuttgart main station from a head to a through station—**'Stuttgart 21'**. The station along with the rail network is to be moved underground and connected to the airport. In addition, a new high-speed line from Wendlingen to Ulm is to be built. Stuttgart 21 is projected to cost around 4.1 billion euros according to current plans, the new line Wendlingen-Ulm 2.9 billion euros. The mega-project has been debated by politicians, planners and citizens for many years.*

Stuttgart 21 divides Stuttgart and agitates Baden-Württemberg. Supporters and opponents have so far seemed irreconcilable. Since the demolition work on the north wing of Stuttgart main station began, the protests against Stuttgart 21 have increased. In the eyes of many citizens, S21 was associated with more ecological, geological and financial risks than economic opportunities. At a demonstration on 30 September [2010], the protest movement confronted the police, resulting in over 100 injuries, including two serious injuries.

Two attempts to bring supporters and opponents of the project together in order to de-escalate the situation failed. Only after the appointment of Heiner Geißler as S21 mediator did the dialogue restart.

It was clear that the mediation's result could not have a legal but a psychological and political binding. Citizen initiatives, politicians and railway board members had gathered and talked to each other. For the first time, the debate was conducted on equal footing. The mediation created transparency which the proceedings had previously lacked. Interested citizens could follow the mediation on television and on the Internet. The complete reasoning of both sides could be presented to an audience of millions.

After the mediation, the mood in Baden-Württemberg has turned in favor of S21. A representative survey commissioned by SWR and Stuttgarter Zeitung showed that by now, 54% of those surveyed in Baden-Württemberg are basically in favor of the project while 38% are against it. On 1 December, a day after Geißler's mediator's speech, Infratest dimap had surveyed 1,010 eligible voters in the federal state by telephone.

Heiner Geißler's arbitrator's award

An important goal of the mediation was to regain credibility and more trust in democracy through depoliticization and a new form of direct democracy.

While there is a quite attractive alternative—head station 21 ("K12")—it has rather specific disadvantages. The most serious disadvantage would be that, from today's point of view, the realization of head station 21 cannot be assumed to be safe, because there has not been sufficient planning and therefore there are no planning approvals and building permits available. Furthermore, financing is not resolved, since the costs for K21 would be estimated differently.

For Stuttgart 21, however, there is a building permit which is equivalent to a right to build for Deutsche Bahn AG. Construction of Stuttgart 21 would not be executed only if Deutsche Bahn AG would voluntarily waive it.

Geißler said that a compromise between Stuttgart 21 and a head station 21 was impossible. However, the opponents' legitimate criticism must be taken into account when planning S21. Geißler believes it is right to continue Stuttgart 21. Deutsche Bahn has the right to build. On a withdrawal from Stuttgart 21, project sponsors, especially Deutsche Bahn AG, would incur high costs, which the opponents of S21 put at 600 million euros and the railway at just under 2.8 billion euros. Stuttgart 21 should be transformed into ***Stuttgart 21 Plus*** *by taking into account the mediation's suggestions.*

Geißler presented his improvement proposals for S21, which, according to him, were accepted by both parties:

1. *The land freed up by the track removal must be transferred to a foundation and taken away from speculation.*
2. *The trees in the palace park (Schlossgarten) are preserved and, if possible, transplanted.*
3. *The Gäubahn remains.*
4. *The suggestions of the Stuttgart fire department for fire protection measures are taken into account at the underground station.*
5. *The planned underground station's safety is to be significantly improved by Deutsche Bahn AG. S21 will be equipped to be barrier-free and accessible for the disabled.*
6. *The underground station must be expanded by a ninth and tenth track. In addition, there will be a two-track westward connection of the airport station to the new line as well as a two-track and non-intersecting 'Wendlinger curve'.*
7. *Deutsche Bahn AG undertakes to carry out a stress test to demonstrate the projected 30% increase in station capacity during peak hour.*

A construction stop until the federal state elections was rejected by both the government and Deutsche Bahn AG. It is to be expected that the protests will continue despite S 21 Plus.

Geißler stated that the mediation as such, the manner of discussion, had been much appreciated by the citizenry. He expressed his wish that the Stuttgart model of democracy would be disseminated throughout Germany. "Landeszentrale für Politische Bildung (Federal State Agency for Civic Education)"

In addition to the methods of participation, conflict resolution and balancing of interests, there are activation methods suitable to encourage actors to common collective action.

4.2.5 Activation Methods

Activation methods are based on an system's increase in redundancy. Instead of aiming for effectiveness and efficiency. Activation methods are about creating space and opportunities, reminiscent of the motto "let a thousand flowers bloom". How this can turn out in practice is shown using the example of the Lower Saxony Youth Initiative Competition "Youth Team-Contest".

The Lower Saxony Youth Initiative Competition "Youth Team-Contest 03104"

The Lower Saxony Youth Initiative Competition "Youth Team-Contest 03104" was carried out by the Youth Association of Paritätischer Niedersachsen e.V. The project's aim was to support self-organization processes of youth initiatives in Lower Saxony and to contribute to the building of social and symbolic capital. For this purpose, an employee was available who, following the governance approach, supported 300 young people aged eight to 30 in 25 initiatives. Five of the youth initiatives had adolescents with individual impairments and/or social disadvantages among their members. These were adolescents from disadvantaged neighborhoods and/or with a migrant background.

If they want to actively promote self-help initiatives of young people, government actors must:

1. In a first step, "examine and possibly change the structures of the social environment or its control parameters". As long as the control parameters of a system are stable, the system remains stable. Only when the control parameters of a social environment change can the structures of the social environment change. The life world of young people has changed and the media environment has gained importance. But not only the life world and the interests of young people, but also those of society have changed, keywords are: PISA debate, education debate, etc. It is necessary to take notice of and use these changes in the social environment, just as with changes at the institutional level. For example, when faced with scarce municipal finances, municipalities develop an interest in self-organization processes of young people, insofar as these are cheaper than external organizations run by employed social workers.
2. In a second step, it is necessary to take advantage of "instability points in the social environment" as a chance for change, because every instability is a "push button" in the sense of governance.
3. In a third step, it is necessary to provide or secure free spaces for young people so that self-organized "youth work folders" can develop (cf. Kolhoff, 2000) (Fig. 4.8).

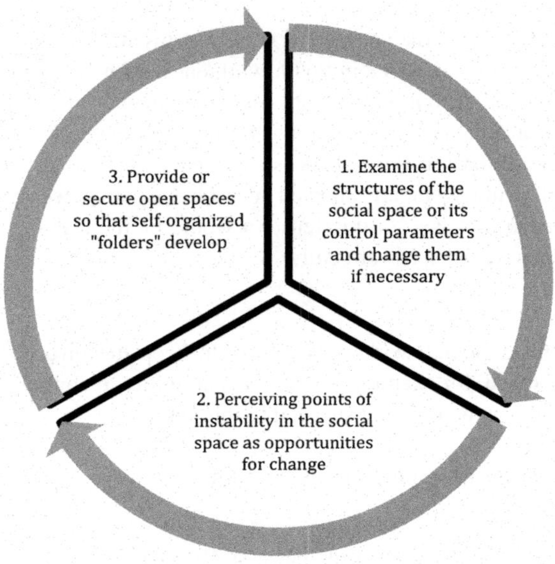

Fig. 4.8 Three steps in promoting self-help initiatives

I. **Changing control parameters as a possible course of action in the social environment**

The fact that self-organization processes of adolescents quickly reach their limits if the control parameters of social space cannot be influenced, was observed, for example, by the initiative "Midnight Sports" in the Lower Saxon community of Bleckede, which took part in the Lower Saxon youth initiative competition. In this initiative, young people had joined forces to pursue sports in a self-determined and self-organized manner outside of externally organized club or association structures. The initiative met with a positive response. The young organizers recruited important actors from the region and were allowed to use a small municipal gym. At the same time, they were not only appreciated within their peer group, but also by outgroups, like the actors in youth work or the press. The young organizers built social and symbolic capital. So equipped, they took into consideration a large school gym and a school sports ground, which they considered to be hardly used. Here, however, they reached the limits of their social space: They were banned from the sports ground. The school's principal pointed out that the sports field was a school facility and therefore only to be used for school activities. Social workers found themselves unable to help the initiative. Schooling is the purview of federal states and so it is here that the influence of municipal actors in youth work ends. Although social workers can appeal to the school and possibly use instruments of public relations to try to initiate changes, their options are limited. They only gain in scope when the control parameters of the social space change. For example, if schools and youth work are allowed to access existing resources with a common action mandate. In this sense, it would be the task of governance to develop new social space structures on a legal regional level, too.

On the other hand, social workers could try to keep the involved actors in an unstable balance and, for example, try to reach an informal compromise via interpersonal networks, which did not succeed in this case.

II. **Instability points as opportunities for change**

In another example from Team-Contest 03104, a youth group had to give up their youth club on the top floor of a village community house due to building code regulations. The control parameters of the social space had changed. In this situation, the young people discovered an old toilet building. They demanded funds for renovating and converting the toilet building into a youth club and used the same building code arguments that the municipal building inspection had used for the closure of their old club.

As is well known, each instability point is an opportunity for change and a "push button" for governance to be aware of and use.

In the example described, the young people and their supporters were able to use the instability point in a positive fashion and initiate a new stable state. The toilet building was converted and is now used as a youth club. Here, too, young people in particular developed social and symbolic capital.

Changes do not always come about spontaneously. Therefore, one of the tasks of governance is to initiate instabilities—one also speaks of disturbances (Piaget, 1974) or perturbations (Maturana & Varela, 1987). For example, a perfectly prepared youth center is unattractive to many young people. In terms of the development of identity, self-esteem and group affiliation, unfinished spaces are much more attractive, since they can be designed by young people themselves and are finished only when these young people enter adulthood. The next generation of young people needs unfinished spaces again, a place to design, to develop their own social and symbolic capital.

III. Create free spaces, facilitate doing things and let folders develop

New structures of social space require new suitable solutions or "germs" (germ cell). Governance should assist in the development of such approaches and support the development of new "germs" of youth work in social space. In the spirit of "Let a thousand flowers bloom", the first step is to make things possible, according to the motto "The more diverse, the better".

1. This requires not only free space, but also a certain tranquility. Youth work that wants to support self-organization processes of young people must also be able to leave the young people in peace.
2. In a second step, "germs" should be supported. They are not rigid, which means they react to disturbances and can adapt to changed conditions, but at the same time, they also have an inner stability and cannot be appropriated.

Only suitable, flexible and yet partially stable models that have developed themselves in social space can become future folders of youth work in the region. Consequently, initiatives of young people, which cannot be given up so easily and also cannot be appropriated so easily, should be supported.

Germs of youth work supposed to become folders, such as those brought to life by the initiative competition (see above), only have a chance if they are supported and

3. their concepts are reflected back into the system of youth work.

In this way, locally developed approaches and ideas can only spread regionally if other young people or actors in youth work learn about them.

> Within the framework of the Team-Contest, the initiatives were therefore provided with instruments of public relations. They took part in media workshops, developed social, symbolic and cultural capital and spread their ideas through the press and television. In addition, some initiatives were able to introduce themselves in a film produced within the framework of the Team-Contest (Hasenbein et al., 2004). This film was made available to other initiatives and actors in youth work in Lower Saxony on DVD.

Festivals, too, play an important role in activating self-organization projects. They deepen the feeling of being connected to others through common concerns.

> The International Building Exhibition accompanied forms of participation with festivals in the 1980s. A particularly fascinating concert was one for a violin and 45 swing grinders. This concert took place on Kreuzberger Admiralstraße. Self-help projects had settled here and in the mid-1980s they were working hard. Admiralstraße was scaffolded and served as a backdrop for a concert for a violin and 45 sanders on a warm summer night. A violin began to play and was illuminated. Opposite, a sander answered and sprayed glowing sparks into the dark summer sky. Another sander answered, until 45 sanders developed a strange concert. The whole thing became a self-help happening.

Within governance, the task is to move different actors to collective action. Joint action requires that a corresponding need for action that cannot be satisfied by individual action is recognized by many actors. Governance only makes sense and can contribute only if joint action is desired. How this can be effectively influenced and shaped in practice is made clear in the following interview:

"Governance in Practice"

"Let me give you an example. We started our training projects, 10 in total, as I said, by selecting groups that seemed interesting to us, so employers, job center, youth area, school area, and teachers, parents, students, who else was there?

Companies …

We simply gathered representatives from all companies, etc., … And democratically chose whom we could grab hold of at the moment. Then we locked them in a room and in a first workshop only sold the message that there is something to do, and we want to do it on a practical, very pragmatic, low-threshold level and we gave them a rule of the game, namely, we all together look for concrete projects. These projects are presented, get a certain time frame, and then they get a decision grid. Then we sent these people home and said, each of you is now asked to submit projects. We did not expect that one would do it, and this calculation has worked out, but we just did it ourselves. These … and others actually came about in my office on a creative afternoon between the two of us. Then we prepared them all in a homogenized form, called a working group, thanked everyone for the many good suggestions that were submitted, and then …, then we said, we anonymize who sent them in and then discussed each individual proposal, 15 min, and then voted, according to a very specific, very simple decision-making pattern: If there were three who raised their finger and say, yes, I am for it and want to get involved in a working group myself, then it was accepted, and if no three were found, who say, yes, I want to invest work, it failed. And then, in the presentation, we pesented one, where we were sure that three supportes would raise their finger, especially since we had identified them before, and we presened one, of which we were sure that it did not have three supporters, so that it was made clear that not every proposal would simply be waved through. And the others we left to themselves a little, and in that way we, I think, during three working group sessions, went through about 15, 16, 17 projects and we identified 10 of them that should be done and then also taught four, five, six something like that to walk step by step. And then the topic was over at some point, so, we could have continued, but as I said, it was a management decision not to continue, but that was an approach on how to get people, let's say, to participate, and they must never take your foot off the pedal, so you have to … the one who is interested is always the one who invites. You have to set the structure, you have to think like the others think,

You only need to ask yourself, who invites me?, I sit there, hopefully no work comes my way. What has to happen so that I am still ready to contribute? So I have to motivate him somehow, it has to be interesting for him. To whom is this interesting? So then he also has to work. How do I get him to work? They have to structure everything beforehand, and they have to help chance along in such a work group, and they have to show the group next time too, that was already … we said that as a starting point, we promised it, we fulfilled it, there we are, how are initial successes, and look, you are on the poster. Of those who see them down there on the posters, many have hardly done anything actively black under the fingernails for the projects, but we invited them to stand on it, because then they are definitely already for it and no longer against it. There are a lot of things, and there is … we have the know-how that we have acquired ourselves, certainly somewhere in there also some value and also describes what such a piece of our success structure was." (Kolhoff, 2010, p. 220)

The example described above can be understood, depending on the point of view, as manipulation or as a clever method, with which the initiators succeeded in structuring a governance arrangement.

4.3 Control Questions for Chap. 4

4.1 What is meant by "Open Space Method"?
4.2 What is meant by "World Café Method"?
4.3 What do you understand by "Future Conference"?
4.4 What do you understand by "Design Thinking"?
4.5 What do you understand by "Mediation Method"?
4.6 How can "Self-Organization Processes" be promoted?

References

Agonda. (2009–2016). Dialog und Zukunftsprozesse, Zukunftskonferenz nach Marvin Weisbord & Sandra Janoff Methode. In: http://agonda.de/zukunftskonferenz/zukunftskonferenz.htm.

Agonda. (Agentur für Dialog und Zukunftsprozesse). Was ist eine Zukunftskonferenz? http://agonda.de/zukunftskonferenz/zukunftskonferenz.html. Zugegriffen: 1. Juli 2021.

Anwaltsplanung bei der Stadtentwicklung in Hannover, zuletzt bearbeitet: 12.06.2013, Autor: Ulrich Rüttgers. http://www.beteiligungskompass.org/article/show/804.

Bürgergutachten Aachen, Aachen 2008, (S. 14–16). http://www.oegut.at/downloads/pdf/p_buergergutachten-aachen.pdf.

Dienel, P. C. (2005). *Die Planungszelle* (5. Aufl.). Westdeutscher Verlag.

Endes, E. (2001), Erfolgsfaktoren des Managements von Netzwerken. Stn. 103 – 121, in: Howald, J., Kopp, R., Flocken, P. (Hrsg.), *Kooperationsverbünde und regionale Modernisierung*. Gabler, Wiesbaden.

FAZ. (2019). Sind wir alle ein bisschen vuca? F.A.Z. – BERUF UND CHANCE, SAMSTAG, 22.06.2019, https://edition.faz.net/faz-edition/beruf-und-chance/2019-0622/150c0b9a76645334f7c382d578b23a50?GEPC=s9.

Hasenbein, F., Mertins, I., & Teams des Youth-Team-Contests 2003/2004 (2004). Jugendinitiativen im Wettbewerb, DVD, Paritätischer Niedersachsen, Hannover.

Häußermann, H., & Siebel, W. (2004). *Stadtsoziologie. Eine Einführung*. Campus.

Herriger, N. (2014). *Empowerment in der Sozialen Arbeit. 5. erweiterte und aktualisierte Aufl.* Kohlhammer.

Heuberger, A. (2007). *Networking – durch interessante Kontakte zum Erfolg*. Cornelsen.

Hinte, W. (2008) Sozialraumorientierung: Ein Fachkonzept für die Soziale Arbeit. Vortrag für den Fachtag Sozialraumorientierung in Fulda am 28.05.2008. http://www.fulda.de/fileadmin/buergerservice/pdf_amt_51/sonstiges/Sozialraumorientierung_Vortrag_W.Hinte_28.5.08.pdf.Zugegriffen: 28. Aug. 2014

Hinte, W., Treeß, H. (2007) *Sozialraumorientierung in der Jugendhilfe*. Juventa-Verl., Weinheim.

Hochschuldidaktik, Methodenbar. https://www.uni-due.de/imperia/md/content/zfh/methodenbar_2012.pdf.

Hofert, S. (2016). *Agiler führen – Einfache Maßnahmen für bessere Teamarbeit, mehr Leistung und höhere Kreativität*. Springer Fachmedien.

HPI Academy (o. J.) Was ist Design Thinking? https://hpi-academy.de/design-thinking/was-ist-design-thinking.html.

Kolhoff, L. (2000). *Schlüsselbegriffe des Systemischen Sozialmanagements* (S. 208–214). Soziale Arbeit 6.

Kolhoff, L. (2010). *Innovationen durchsetzen. Das Konzept der Regional Governance in der Sozialen Arbeit*. (S.217–220). Blätter der Wohlfahrtspflege 6.

Kühl, S. (2009). Visualisierungsmethoden. In Kühl, S., Strodtholz, P., & Taffertshofer, A. (eds). *Handbuch Methoden der Organisationsforschung*. VS Verlag für Sozialwissenschaften.

Kuhn, H. R., (1999), Konflikte systemisch und dynamisch lösen. Nicht der Konflikt ist das Problem, sondern die Unfähigkeit, ihn zu regeln. 5 Schritte zur Klärung von Auseinandersetzungen. (S. 55–64). In Blätter der Wohlfahrtspflege 3 und 4/99.

Kulig, W., Schirbort, K., & Schubert M. (Hrsg.). (2011). *Empowerment behinderter Menschen*. Kohlhammer.

Landeszentrale für Politische Bildung Baden-Württemberg (o. J.). Schlichtung Stuttgart 21. https://www.lpb-bw.de/schlichtung_s21.html. Zugegriffen: 20. Aug. 2019.

Lewin, K. (1953). *Die Lösung sozialer Konflikte*. Christian-Verlag.

Maturana, H. R., & Varela, F. J. (1987). *Der Baum der Erkenntnis*. Scherz.

Piaget, J. (1974). *Biologie und Erkenntnis*. Fischer.

Reich, K. (Hrsg.) (2008). Methodenpool. http://methodenpool.uni-koeln.de. Zugegriffen: 1. Juli 2021.

Schubert, H. (2021). Organisation von Netzwerken in der Sozialwirtschaft – Orientierungsrahmen für das Management. In Kolhoff, L. (Hrsg.), *Aktuelle Diskurse in der Sozialwirtschaft III* (S. 4–24). Springer VS.

Seifert, M. (2012). Schritte zur Inklusion im sozialen Nahraum bei schwerer Behinderung. In Hinz, A., Körner, I. & Niedorf, U. (Hrsg.), *Von der Integration zur Inklusion* (3. Aufl., S. 163–175). Lebenshilfe-Verlag.

Seligmann, M. E. P. (1995). *Erlernte Hilflosigkeit* (3. Aufl.). Beltz.

Sloterdijk, P. (2004). *Sphären* (Bd. 3). Suhrkamp.

Söllner, K. (2010). World Cafe – ein Erfahrungsbericht. https://docplayer.org/47196423-World-cafe-ein-erfahrungsbericht.html. Zugegriffen: 1. Juli 2021.

Speckbacher, G., & Pfaffenzeller, H. (2004). Die Governance von Nonprofit- Organisationen aus Sicht eines ökonomischen Stakeholder-Ansatzes. In Witt, D., Purtschert, R. & Schauer, R. (Hrsg.), *Funktionen und Leistungen von Nonprofit-Organisationen*. 6. Internationales Colloquium der NPO-Forscher. Technische Universität München, 25. und 26. März 2004 (S. 187–212). Deutscher Universitäts-Verlag.

Straus, F. (2004). *Soziale Netzwerke und Sozialraumorientierung – Gemeindepsychologische Anmerkungen zur Sozialraumdebatte*. IPP- Arbeitspapier Nr. 1, München.

Theunissen, G. (2009). *Empowerment und Inklusion behinderter Menschen* (2. Aufl, Freiburg i. Br.: Lambertus).

5 Answers to the Control Questions

In answer to question 1.1: In the economy, transaction costs play an important role. Contracts and agreements have to be negotiated and compliance with the contract has to be ensured. In addition, costs arise when agreements are incomplete or incorrect and have to be corrected. The main factor for low transaction costs is factor specificity, which is based on the criteria of market, cooperation or hierarchy. You do not necessarily achieve an economic advantage when transactions are carried out via the market, hierarchies and networks also play a decisive role. Factor specificity can be explained using an example from the printing industry. While it is crucial for a daily newspaper that the issue arrives in time in the morning, the printing time can be individually negotiated for a book publication and less lucrative offers can be rejected by the publisher. Newspaper publishers usually have their own printing presses, book publishers do not.

In answer to question 1.2: In political science, the concept is defined in order to distinguish it from government. The important point here is the central difference between formal procedures in government systems on the one hand and informal, flexible structures on the other. While government is directed from top to bottom (top-down) and long-term planning has priority, governance is about medium-term, individual negotiation processes, accords and agreements. These processes aim at self-regulation and allow more leeway within networks and cooperation.

The governance approach is particularly relevant in negotiations and agreements across national borders, as it is not just one government that makes decisions, but many stakeholders and representatives from different political structures and power relations who make decisions together. The cooperation of public and non-public actors, that is, representatives from politics and society, who negotiate at different levels, is important, here. This cooperation is controlled

L. Kolhoff, *Governance in the Social Economy*,
https://doi.org/10.1007/978-3-658-38743-3_5

by legal elements (hierarchy), but also by negotiations and political competition. Examples of governance are the open coordination method in the EU or the CETA free trade agreement between the EU and Canada.

In response to question 2.1: "First-order governance" refers to political and economic processes of negotiation and problem-solving, with a focus on local and regional problem-solving and policy processes in the social economy.

In response to question 2.2: An example of local governance is the "Soziale Stadt" (social city) program. This joint project of the federal government and the states is about improving local living conditions, and it includes buildings, infrastructure, but also the strengthening of social coexistence. In local governance, on the one hand, various social actors are involved. In the case of "Soziale Stadt" these are, among others, representatives of schools, employment agencies, housing companies, etc. On the other hand, management is designed in a strategic and cross-sectoral fashion. In order to guarantee the successful implementation of the "Soziale Stadt" program, e.g., work groups are set up for different topics and local networks are activated. Concepts of action developed there are then presented to representatives from politics and administration. Coordination, steering and implementation groups are set up to control.

In response to question 2.3: "Regional Governance" is about complex organizational forms for specific regions. Regions are sections of a state which comprise a larger area than a city or municipality. Examples of "Regional Governance" are the International Building Exhibition "Emscher Park" or the region of Stuttgart. Governance on a regional level is often triggered by the lack of or only little existing state structures, thus the lack of "government" structures. In regional governance, both state and non-state actors with a spatial function come together voluntarily. For example, representatives from business, culture, and labor market policy work together to develop new self-regulation concepts specifically tailored to the region. The goal of regional governance is to strengthen trust, solidarity, public welfare orientation, and willingness to cooperate in a limited local area. The regional forms of self-regulation are based on voluntary participation.

In response to question 2.4: "Second-Order-Governance" includes institutional framework conditions of governance.

In response to question 2.5: The "welfare mix" is about the interplay of the four sectors state, market, intermediary sector (also called third sector or nonprofit sector) and informal sector. The state acts through public administration and is structured by law and hierarchy. The market is dominated by companies and governed by money and competition. In the intermediary sector, clubs, associations and foundations are active and the structure is created and maintained through communication and voluntariness. The informal sector is coordinated by families and communities through personal relationships and obligations. The four sectors shaping the welfare mix are interwoven and cooperate in complex structures.

In response to question 2.6: In the activating welfare state, the state has increasingly withdrawn to a guarantee function and included the other sectors—the market, the intermediary and the informal sector—in the procurement of social benefits. For example, an increasing reliance is placed on the commitment of volunteers and family members.

In response to question 2.7: There were changes from the "democratic state" to an "active and lean state" and then to an "activating state".

In response to question 2.8: Governance is to be understood in contrast to the efficiency-oriented "New Public Management" approach, which is aimed at customer satisfaction and quality, but could not be successfully transferred to bureaucratic structures. In contrast to "New Public Management", governance in administrative processes aims at the participation and engagement of employees, rather than directing them from above and telling them what to do.

In response to question 2.9: Governance has gained importance in the field of state planning. Political planning approaches of the 60s and 70s with ministries as the main designers have included just as little civic engagement as the subsequent steering approaches via large actors such as associations, parties and administrations. In contrast, governance in planning claims to promote the self-organization of society and institutions. For example, the higher education system has been controlled to a lesser extent by laws, ordinances and decrees for some time.

In response to question 2.10: "Third-Order-Governance" includes normative guidelines, rules and standards.

In response to question 2.11: The origin of the "Good Governance Approach" is the World Bank's Africa study of 1989. It was recognized that economic assistance is not fruitful if it is not managed and controlled by functioning institutions.

In order to ensure "Good Governance", firstly, the public administration must be efficiently structured, secondly, both important social groups and minorities must be involved in decision-making and thirdly, clear relationships between public and private sector must be established in order to combat corruption and nepotism or to prevent them.

In response to question 3.1: The term arose after a number of British corporate collapses in the 1990s. It became increasingly common for managers of individual companies, the so-called "agents", to pursue their own interests that did not coincide with those of the owner, the "principal" (principal-agent conflict).

In response to question 3.2: The "Corporate Governance Code" is intended, inter alia, to strengthen confidence in the management of listed companies by making the role of the board of directors, the cooperation with the supervisory board and other issues relevant to accounting and auditing more transparent to the outside.

In response to question 3.3: In the non-profit sector, for example, the interests of the board of directors (comparable to the principals) can diverge from those of the management (comparable to the agents). In addition to the board of directors and management, which are comparable to principal-agent structures in the private sector, external stakeholders such as funders are added in the social economy.

In response to question 3.4: Natural networks include, for example, family circles (primary networks) or school classes (secondary networks). Natural networks are characterized by the fact that they are not or only slightly structured and one is born or socialized into them. Artificial (tertiary) networks are cooperation between institutions that were founded for a specific purpose.

In response to question 3.5: The most important means of establishing common structures of action is to trust each other and to share common values and experiences in the network.

In response to question 3.6: Not all organizations are open and receptive to a network. The judiciary was given as an example. Cooperation is often seen as hindering or endangering neutrality in adjudication. Another example was the cooperation between police and social work. While the police are concerned with securing public life, social work is focused on inclusion. That there are different interests can be illustrated by the example of "shooting galleries" where drug addicts can inject substances. While the consumption of illegal drugs is sanctioned by the police, the aid of the "shooting galleries" pursues the goal of offering someone who is addicted hygienic conditions and counseling.

In response to question 3.7: Cooperation is only possible if internal structures are created that allow a connection. If this is not the case, networks strongly depend on individuals and the success of network structures depends above all on the personal position of the actors in the respective organizations and institutions. Neutrality and objectivity as well as authenticity and communication skills are important key qualifications here.

In response to question 3.8: The interests of governance actors from politics, business and associations can be very different. For example, politicians usually have the goal of being re-elected and must weigh which issues they will place on their political agenda. In this context, one speaks of the action logic of power. A company, on the other hand, wants to achieve the highest possible profit and therefore acts according to the logics of market and price. Associations, in turn, follow professional logics or those of association politics.

In response to question 3.9: The key factors for successful cooperation are communication and trust, as well as shared goals and visions. The "chemistry" must be right so that governance functions as a decision-making process. It is crucial that governance is always based on voluntary cooperation. For the participants of governance processes, it is decisive that the benefits are greater than the costs. That is why governance structures can also quickly break down if, for example, conflicts flare up and the effort or commitment is greater than the result.

In response to question 3.10: In decision-making, it is often not the formal resolution, but the corresponding preparation processes that are decisive. It must be asked where, when and in which committees preliminary decisions are made and, above all, under the influence of which persons.

In response to question 3.11: The "degree of connection" is the degree of networking and an indicator of the social capital of a person. The greater and/or more intense the number of contacts a person has, the greater their social capital.

In response to question 4.1: Open space, or "free space", is a participatory method for groups of 8 to 1,000 people. The open space method serves self-organization. There is a main topic, but no fixed framework: The framework for this topic is designed in the group. The method serves the quick and creative problem solving.

In response to question 4.2: The name "World Café" goes back to a relaxed "coffee house atmosphere". As in the coffee house, the participants should feel comfortable and let their creativity run free. The method is suitable for up to 2,000 participants who use describable tablecloths for their ideas at different tables for about 2–3 h. There are guiding questions that are discussed at the tables in different group constellations. Each table has a host who summarizes the previous rounds of conversation and animates the newly assembled conversation partners to discuss the guiding questions again. The result is a reflection phase.

For question 4.3: The future conference, which is suitable for smaller group constellations (approx. 60–80 people), works on a common future scenario and action steps on three days which bring them closer to this scenario. Day 1 is about finding out together where one stands, what connects the group and what one can expect in the future. On day 2, the participants deal with positive examples of the present and already identify common future visions. Day 3 is used to concretize this common idea of the future and to develop central action steps to get there together.

For question 4.4: Design Thinking is a new approach to problem solving in which participants from different fields come together and try to develop products from the user's perspective.

For question 4.5: Mediation is an effective method for conflict resolution and balancing interests. While conficts that are resolved legally are about victory or defeat, the goal of a mediation procedure is to develop a common solution. The mediator acts as a neutral intermediary and creates a conversation atmosphere that is used by the conflict parties to develop their own solutions. Mediation is a constructive conciliation process that can be used in conflicts between two individuals, but also between groups and institutions. A prerequisite for the success of the method is that the conflict parties have a serious interest in finding a solution and choose the mediation approach voluntarily and are not forced to do so. It is about the joint further development and the development of a win-win situation for all involved.

In response to question 4.6: The example of the Lower Saxony Youth Initiative Competition "Youth Team-Contest 03104" can be used to explain how self-organization processes can be promoted. In a first step, first of all, consideration must be given to social and institutional changes, secondly, points of instability in the social environment should be located as opportunities for development and, thirdly, spaces for self-organization should be provided or secured. (Especially with youth projects, it is about a certain "unfinishedness" and space for own design.) The task of governance is to trigger these processes. Flexibility is needed, but also a certain stability, so that self-organization processes can be successful.

References

Aachen Declaration of the German Association of Towns and Municipalities on the occasion of the congress "Education in the City" on 22./23. November 2007. https://www.staedtetag.de/files/dst/docs/Dezernat-3/Archiv/aachener-erklaerung-2007.pdf. Accessed: 05. Apr. 2021.

Agonda (Agentur für Dialog und Zukunftsprozesse). What is a future conference? http://agonda.de/zukunftskonferenz/zukunftskonferenz.html. Accessed: 01. July 2021.

Arnig, N. (21. April 2008). In the name of the citizen. *Frankfurter Rundschau.*

Auer, J. (2010). Helpful also for small organizations – The code of lebenshilfe has proven itself. *Blätter der Wohlfahrtspflege 6,* 211 et seq.

Bachert, R. (2006). What does corporate governance mean? In R. Bachert (Hrsg.), *Corporate Governance in Nonprofit-Unternehmen* (P. 14–26). WRS Verlag.

Bachert, R. (Ed.). (2006). *Corporate governance in nonprofit organizations.* WRS-Verlag.

Bangert, C. (2010). Separate management and supervision – the principles of responsible corporate governance in the German Caritas Association. *Blätter der Wohlfahrtspflege 6,* 207–210.

Baums, T. (Ed.). (2001). *Report of the government commission on corporate governance: Management, corporate control, modernization of stock corporation law.* O. Schmidt.

Beck, M. (2010). Managing organizations well and correctly. *Blätter der Wohlfahrtspflege 6,* 203–206.

Becker, T., Dammer, I., Howaldt, J., & Loose, A. (2011). *Network management.* Springer.

Benz, A. (Ed.). (2004). *Governance – Governing in complex rule systems* (1st Ed.). VS Verlag.

Benz, A., & Dose, N. (2010). Governance – Fashion term or useful social science concept. In A. Benz & N. Dose (Eds.), *Governance – Governing in complex rule systems* (2nd updated and revised Ed., pp. 13–36). VS Verlag.

Benz, A., Lütz, S., Schimank, U., & Simonis, G. (Eds.). (2007). *Handbook of Governance.* VS Verlag.

Bougmil, J., & Holtkamp, L. (2004). Local governance and social integration. In S. Lange & U. Schimank (Hrsg.), *Governance and social integration* (S. 147–166). VS Verlag.

Bullinger, H., & Nowak, J. (1998). *Social network work. An introduction for social professions.* Lambertus.

L. Kolhoff, *Governance in the Social Economy,*
https://doi.org/10.1007/978-3-658-38743-3

Federal Institute for Research on Building, Urban Affairs and Spatial Development (BBSR) in the Federal Office for Building and Regional Planning (BBR) (Ed.). (2020). *Study Local Economy BIWAQ. ESF Federal Programme "Education, Economy, Employment in the Neighbourhood – BIWAQ" – Final Project Report. Bonn.*

Federal Ministry of the Interior, Building and Home Affairs (BMI). (2019). 20 years of integrated urban development. The Social City. https://www.bmi.bund.de/SharedDocs/downloads/DE/publikationen/themen/bauen/wohnen/20-jahre-soziale-stadt.pdf?__blob=publicationFile&v=3.

Federal Ministry of the Interior, Building and Home Affairs (BMI). (2021). Social City. https://www.staedtebaufoerderung.info/StBauF/DE/Programm/SozialeStadt/soziale_stadt_node.html.

Federal Ministry of the Interior, Building and Home Affairs (BMI). (2019), Social City. The urban development programme for disadvantaged urban and rural areas. https://www.sozialestadt.de.

Citizen's Report Aachen, Aachen 2008, pp. 14–16. http://www.oegut.at/downloads/pdf/p_buergergutachten-aachen.pdf.

Castells, M. (2017). *The rise of the network society. The information age, economy, society, culture, Volume 1* (2nd Ed.). Springer VS.

Corporate Governance Code Good corporate governance in the life assistance. A recommendation of the Federal Association of Life Assistance for People with Intellectual Disabilities e.V. for their member organizations, as of summer 2012 Source: https://www.lebenshilfe.de/de/ueber-uns/aufgaben-und-ziele/Dateien/06-Corporate-Governance-Kodex-Lebenshilfe.php?listLink=1.

Czada, R. (2010). Good governance as a concept for government action: Basics, applications, criticism. In A. Benz & N. Dose (Eds.), *Governance – governing in complex rule systems* (2nd updated and revised Ed.). VS Verlag.

Deutscher Bundestag. (2005). Bericht über die Lebenssituation junger Menschen und die Leistungen der Kinder- und Jugendhilfe in Deutschland – Zwölfter Kinder- und Jugendbericht – Deutscher Bundestag Drucksache 15/6014 15. Wahlperiode 10.10.2005. http://dip21.bundestag.de/dip21/btd/15/060/1506014.pdf. Accessed: 05. Apr. 2021.

Dienel, P. C. (2005). *Die Planungszelle* (5. Aufl.). Westdeutscher Verlag.

difu (Deutsches Institut für Urbanistik) (Jekel, G. unter Mitarbeit von Beckmann, K. J., Arndt, P., Müller, K., Sander, R., Scheumann, D.) im Auftrag der Senatsverwaltung für Stadtentwicklung, Berlin. (2007). *Vorstudie zur Einrichtung einer „Netzwerkagentur Generationenübergreifendes Wohnen", Sonderveröffentlichungen.* http://edoc.difu.de/edoc.php?id=COZ7M16W. Accessed: 19. Aug. 2019.

Eberle, D. (2010). Governance in der politischen Ökonomie II: Corporate Governance. In A. Benz & N. Dose (Hrsg.), *Governance – Regieren in komplexen Regelsystemen* (2., aktualisierte und veränderte Aufl., S. 155–173). VS Verlag.

Europäische Kommission. (2001). *Europäisches Regieren*. Weißbuch, Amt für amtliche Veröffentlichungen der Europäischen Gemeinschaften.

Evers, A., & Olk, T. (1996). Welfare pluralism. Analytical and normative-political dimensions of a leading concept. In A. Evers & T. Olk (Eds.), *Welfare pluralism. From the welfare state to the welfare society* (pp. 9–62). Westdeutscher Verlag.

FAZ. (2019). Are we all a little vuca? F.A.Z. - BERUF UND CHANCE. https://edition.faz.net/faz-edition/beruf-und-chance/2019-0622/150c0b9a76645334f7c382d-578b23a50?GEPC=s9. Accessed: 22. June 2019.

Florian, F. (2008). Network work. The network perspective in practice. In H. Schubert (Ed.), *Network management.* VS Verlag.

Fürst, D. (2007). Regional governance. In A. Benz, S. Lütz, U. Schimank, & G. Simonis (Eds.), *Handbook governance* (pp. 353–650). VS Verlag.

Fürst, D. (2010). Regional governance. In A. Benz & N. Dose (Eds.), *Governance – Regieren in komplexen Regelsystemen* (2nd, updated and revised Ed., pp. 49–68). VS Verlag.

Fürst, D. (2004). Regional Governance. In A. Benz (Hrsg.), *Governance – Regieren in komplexen Regelsystemen* (1. Aufl., S. 45–64). VS Verlag.

Garcia Sanz, F. J., Semmler, K., & Walther, J. (Hrsg.). (2007). *Die Automobilindustrie auf dem Weg zur globalen Netzwerkkompetenz. Effiziente und flexible Supply Chains erfolgreich gestalten.* Springer-Verlag.

Greca, R. (2005). Local governance in the age of globalization – a new myth? In L. Kolhoff, R. Beck, H.D. Engelhardt, M. Hege, & J. Sandmann (Eds.), *Between economy and social responsibility* (pp. 50–82). Ziel.

Handelsblatt from 13.10.2015.

Hasenbein, F., Mertins, I., & Teams of the Youth-Team-Contests 2003/2004 (2004). *Youth Initiatives in Competition.* DVD.

Häußermann, H., & Siebel, W. (2004). *Stadtsoziologie. Eine Einführung.* Campus.

Häußermann, H., & Walther, U.-J. (2018). Soziale Stadt, In ARL – Akademie für Raumforschung und Landesplanung (Ed.), *Handwörterbuch der Stadt- und Raumentwicklung* (S. 2197–2206). ARL – Akademie für Raumforschung und Landesplanung, ISBN 978-3-88838-559-9. http://nbn-resolving.de/urn:nbn:de:0156-55992035.

Heinrich-Böll-Stiftung. (Hrsg.). (2011). Kommunale Bildungslandschaften. Ein Bericht von Anika Duveneck und Einblicke in die Praxis von Sybille Volkholz, Reihe Bildung und Kultur, Band 9. https://www.boell.de/sites/default/files/2012-02-Kommunale_Bildungslandschaften.pdf. Zugegriffen: 05. Apr. 2021.

Herriger, N. (2014). *Empowerment in der Sozialen Arbeit* (5. erweiterte und aktualisierte Aufl.). Kohlhammer.

Heuberger, A. (2007). *Networking – durch interessante Kontakte zum Erfolg.* Cornelsen.

Hinte, W. (2005) Von der Gemeinwesenarbeit über die Stadtteilarbeit zur Initiierung bürgerschaftlichen Engagements. In W. Thole (Hrsg.), *Grundriss Soziale Arbeit* (2. Aufl., S. 535–548). VS Verlag.

Hinte, W. (2008). Sozialraumorientierung: Ein Fachkonzept für die Soziale Arbeit. Vortrag für den Fachtag Sozialraumorientierung in Fulda am 28.05.2008. http://www.fulda.de/fileadmin/buergerservice/pdf_amt_51/ sonstiges/Sozialraumorientierung_Vortrag_W.Hinte_28.5.08.pdf. Zugegriffen: 28. Aug. 2014.

Hinte, W., & Treeß, H. (2007). *Sozialraumorientierung in der Jugendhilfe.* Juventa-Verlag.

Higher Education Didactics, Methodenbar. https://www.uni-due.de/imperia/md/content/zfh/methodenbar_2012.pdf.

Hofert, S. (2016). *Agiler führen – Einfache Maßnahmen für bessere Teamarbeit, mehr Leistung und höhere Kreativität.* Springer Fachmedien.

HPI Academy. (o. J.). Was ist Design Thinking? https://hpi-academy.de/design-thinking/was-ist-design-thinking.html.

Jann, W., & Wegrich, K. (2010). Governance und Verwaltungspolitik: Leitbilder und Reformkonzepte. In A. Benz & N. Dose (Hrsg.), *Governance – Regieren in komplexen Regelsystemen* (2., aktualisierte und veränderte Aufl., S. 175–200). VS Verlag.

Kolhoff, L. (2000). Schlüsselbegriffe des Systemischen Sozialmanagements. *Soziale Arbeit 6,* 208–214.

Kolhoff, L. (2010). Innovationen durchsetzen. Das Konzept der Regional Governance in der Sozialen Arbeit. *Blätter der Wohlfahrtspflege 6,* 217–220.

Kolhoff, L., & Gebhardt, C. (Hrsg.). (2016). *Stadtteil in der Schule.* Springer VS.

Kooiman, J. (2003). *Governing as governance.* Sage Publications Ltd.

Kühl, S. (2009) Visualization methods. In S. Kühl, P. Strodtholz, & A. Taffertshofer (Eds.), *Handbook of methods of organization research.* VS Verlag.

Kuhn, H. R. (1999). *Resolving Conflicts Systemically and Dynamically. It is not the conflict that is the problem, but the inability to resolve it. 5 steps to clarifying disputes* (pp. 55–64). Blätter der Wohlfahrtspflege 3 and 4/99.

Kulig, W., Schirbort, K., & Schubert, M. (Hrsg.). (2011). *Empowerment behinderter Menschen.* Kohlhammer.

Landeszentrale für Politische Bildung Baden-Württemberg. (o. J.). Schlichtung Stuttgart 21. https://www.lpb-bw.de/schlichtung_s21.html. Zugegriffen: 20. Aug. 2019.

Lawyer planning in urban development in Hanover, last edited: 12.06.2013, author: Ulrich Rüttgers. http://www.beteiligungskompass.org/article/show/804.

Lewin, K. (1953). *Die Lösung sozialer Konflikte.* Christian-Verlag.

Luthe, E.W. (2009). *Municipal education landscapes. Legal and organizational foundations.* Erich Schmidt Verlag GmbH & Co.

Marschik, N. (2016). Anlagen zur Allgemeinen Erhebung in den Sozialräumen der Grundschule Altmühlstraße, Rheinring und Bebelhof. In L. Kolhoff & C. Gebhardt (Hrsg.), *Stadtteil in der Schule* (S. 234–239). Springer VS.

Maturana, H. R., & Varela, F. J. (1987). *The Tree of Knowledge.* Scherz.

Mayntz, R. (2010). Governance in the modern state. In A. Benz & N. Dose (Eds.), *Governance - Governing in complex rule systems* (2nd, updated and revised Ed., pp. 37–48). VS Verlag.

Milotay, N. (2017). Social governance in the European Union. Governing complex systems. European Parliamentary Research Service PE 614.579. https://www.europarl.europa.eu/RegData/etudes/IDAN/2017/614579/EPRS_IDA(2017)614579_EN.pdf. Accessed: 18. Apr. 2021.

Mitchell, R. K., Agle, B. R., & Wood, D. J. (1997). Toward a theory of stakeholder identification and salience: Defining the principle of who and what really counts. *Academy of Management Review, 22nd year,* (4), 853–896.

Piaget, J. (1974). *Biology and knowledge.* Fischer.

Rakebrandt, D. (2006). *Regional Governance in Youth Work Illustrated by the Example of the Region Verden.* unpublished Master's thesis at the FH Braunschweig/Wolfenbüttel, Master's programme in Social Management.

Reich, K. (Ed.) (2008). Methodenpool. https://methodenpool.uni-koeln.de. Accessed: 01. July 2021.

Riege, M., Schubert, H. (Eds.). (2019). *Sozialraumanalyse. Grundlagen – Methoden – Praxis* (6th unchanged Ed.). Verlag Sozial – Raum – Management.

Roß, P. S. (2018). Governance. In K. Grunwald & A. Langer (Hrsg.), *Social Economics. Handbook for Science and Practice* (S. 726–738). Nomos.

Schubert H. (2018a). *Network orientation in municipality and social economy. An introduction.* Springer VS.

Schubert, H. (2018b). *Network management in municipality and social economy. An introduction.* Springer VS.

Schubert, H. (2018). *Network orientation in municipality and social economy.* Springer VS.

Schubert, H. (2021). Organisation von Netzwerken in der Sozialwirtschaft – Orientierungsrahmen für das Management. In L. Kolhoff (Hrsg.), *Aktuelle Diskurse in der Sozialwirtschaft III* (S. 4–24). Springer VS.

Schubert, H. (Hrsg.). (2008). *Netzwerkmanagement – Koordination von professionellen Vernetzungen – Grundlagen und Praxisbeispiele.* VS Verlag.

Schuhen, A. (2014). Corporate Governance in sozialwirtschaftlichen Organisationen. In U. Arnold, K. Grunwald, & B. Maelicke (Hrsg.), *Lehrbuch der Sozialwirtschaft* (S. 525–545). Nomos.

Seifert, M. (2012). Steps to inclusion in the social environment for people with severe disabilities. In A. Hinz, I. Körner, & U. Niedorf (Eds.), *From integration to inclusion* (3rd Ed., pp. 163–175). Lebenshilfe-Verlag.

Seligmann, M. E. P. (1995). *Learned helplessness* (3rd Ed.). Beltz.

Sloterdijk, P. (2004). *Spheres* (Vol. 3). Suhrkamp.

Söllner, K. (2010). World Cafe – an experience report. https://docplayer.org/47196423-World-cafe-ein-erfahrungsbericht.html. Accessed: 01. July 2021.

Speckbacher, G., & Pfaffenzeller, H. (2004). The governance of nonprofit organizations from the perspective of an economic stakeholder approach. In D. Witt, R. Purtschert & R. Schauer (Eds.), *Functions and services of nonprofit organizations. 6th International Colloquium of NPO Researchers. Technical University of Munich, 25th and 26th March 2004* (pp. 187–212). Deutscher Universitäts-Verlag.

Straus, F. (2004). *Social networks and community-oriented social work - community psychological notes on the debate on social work.* IPP Working Paper No. 1, Munich.

Sydow, J. (1992). *Strategic networks: Evolution and organization.* Gabler.

Sydow, J. (Ed.). (2010). *Management of network organizations: Contributions from "Management Research"* (5th, updated Ed.). Gabler.

Theunissen, G. (2009). *Empowerment and inclusion of disabled people* (2nd ed.). Lambertus.

Theuvsen, L. (2001). Stakeholder management – options for dealing with interest groups, Münsteraner Diskussionspapiere zum Nonprofit-Sektor 16. https://www.aktive-buergerschaft.de/fp_files/Diskussionspapiere/2001wp-band16. Accessed: 10. June 2021.

Vester, F. (1993). *Our world - a networked system* (8th ed.). dtv.

Wald, A., & Jansen, D. (2007). Networks. In A. Benz, S. Lütz, U. Schimank, & G. Simonis (Eds.), *Handbook Governance* (pp. 93–105). VS Verlag.

Weyer, J. (2011). *Social networks. Concepts and methods of social network research. Munich 2000* (2nd Ed.). Oldenbourg.

Williamson, O. E. (1990). *The economic institutions of capitalism.* Mohr.

Yollu-Tok, A. (2016). From the "European Employment Strategy" to the "Open Method of Coordination" in the field of social policy. In P. Hammerschmidt, U. Köttler, & J. Sagebiel, (Eds.), *The European Union and social work* (1st Ed., pp. 79–97). AG SPAK.

Recommended References

Bachert, R. (Ed.). (2006). *Corporate Governance in Nonprofit Organizations.* WRS-Verlag.

Benz, A., Lütz, S., Schimank, U., & Simonis, G. (Eds.). (2007). *Handbook of governance.* VS Verlag.

Benz. A., & Dose, N. (Hrsg.). (2010). *Governance – Regieren in komplexen Regelsystemen* (2., aktualisierte und veränderte Aufl.). VS Verlag.

Evers, A., Heinze, R. G., & Olk, T. (Hrsg.) (2011). *Handbuch Soziale Dienste.* Springer VS.

Lewin, K. (1953). *Die Lösung sozialer Probleme.* Christian.

Schubert, H. (Ed.). (2008). *Network management – coordination of professional networks – basics and practice examples.* VS Verlag.

Schwalb, L., & Walk, H. (Eds.). (2007). *Local governance – More transparency through proximity to citizens?* VS Verlag.

Wendt, W. R. (2010). *Wohlfahrtsarrangements. Neue Wege in der Sozialwirtschaft.* Nomos.

Weyer, J. (2014). *Soziale Netzwerke. Konzepte und Methoden der sozialwissenschaftlichen Netzwerkforschung. München 2000* (3. überarbeitete Aufl.). Oldenbourg Wissenschaftsverlag GmbH.